Discovering America
One Marathon at a Time

Jim Anderson

Discovering America

One Marathon at a Time

© 2015 James D. Anderson.

All rights reserved.

ISBN-13: 978-1516958078

ISBN-10: 1516958071

Published by
James Brakken's
Badger Valley Publishing
45255 East Cable Lake Road
Cable, Wisconsin 54821
715-798-3163

An independent publisher for independent authors.

TreasureofNamakagon@Gmail.com   BadgerValley.com

Denise, Dexter, and the author with the marathon medals

I dedicate this book to my wife Denise. Without her help this journey would not have been completed. She has been with me either physically or through words of encouragement and prayers at every race. Together we completed our goal of running a marathon in every state.

Denise never had to persuade me to keep after the goal but she did have to help keep me from being too critical of myself for not doing well enough in some marathons. I try to live by the idea of doing the best I can and then let it go, but I need her help doing that.

ACKNOWLEDGMENTS

After being told my book was amazingly original by a large publishing company and given many reasons why I should have them publish my book, I realized I needed help with these decisions.

I contacted James Brakken, author and independent publisher. He looked over my manuscript and agreed I had a good book. He and his golden retriever Maddie came over and while Maddie kept Dexter company James helped me finalize my book for the printers. I thank him for his knowledge, experience, and above all, the time he put in to prepare my book for printing.

Chapter	Location	Page

Foreword

Goals. We all set them. Some large. Some not. Most come from within. Some are inspired by others.

Jim Anderson, a Wisconsin public school teacher closing in on retirement, had a fellow tell him, "At your age, you could never run a marathon in every state." Though not meant as a challenge, one marathon soon led to the next and the next. Twelve years later, Anderson crossed yet another finish line, allowing him to join that finite group of determined athletes who have run a marathon in each of our nation's states.

This is more than a book about how to run or where or why or when. True, the struggle to complete these fifty arduous races captures attention. How could it not? But it is the backstory of each event—the people, the history, the charm of each new place— that fascinates. Chapter after chapter presents another atypical look at our land, unique perspectives missed by everyday travelers.

As one who has organized, coordinated, and participated in many athletic competitions, I can say that this book, Jim Anderson's chronicle of discovering America one marathon at a time, is both fascinating and inspiring as well as an amazing goal conquered.

Gary Crandall
Chequamegon Fat Tire Festival Director
2003 Mountain Bike Hall of Fame Inductee

Discovering America
One Marathon at a Time

The Marathon's History

The marathon's history starts during the Greek vs Persian conflict, with the weaker, Greek city-states being under attack by the stronger Persian army. Athens needed Sparta's help to hold off the Persians, so they sent a runner named Phidippides with the message. It was about 140 miles through mountainous terrain to Sparta. He ran it in about a day and a half, or a 15-minute mile average. The Spartans had religious concerns; since they were watching the moon's phase, they would have to delay their help. Phidippides, according to legend, had to run the same distance back to inform the Athenians with the news. The Athenians decided to take on the Persians in a suicide attack.

Legend says Phidippides put on heavy armor to fight in the battle. They were at a four to one disadvantage on the Fields of Marathon. The Persians were shocked by the Athenians taking them on by themselves and lost over 6,000 soldiers in the surprise attack. When the battle was over the aromatic scent of marathon (the Greek word for fennel) was replaced by the putrid smell of bloated Persian bodies rotting in the hot Mediterranean sun. The rest of the Persians headed to the sea to go back and attack Athens before the Athenian army could get back in a defensive position. Phidippides once again, according to legend, was called on to warn Athens of the attack. The legend says he made the 26-mile run in about three hours and fell over dead from exhaustion after he delivered the message.

The first run to Sparta is backed by history. The rest of the Phidippides story is a legend that Superman would have trouble with. The battle happened in 490 BC. The legend developed 600 years after the Persian and Greek War. The marathon as we know it today got its beginning from the legend.

The marathon was introduced into the Olympics in 1898 at a distance of about 25 miles. Later, in 1908, the London games made the marathon 26 miles, the distance from Windsor Castle to White City Stadium. King Edward VII's royal box for the games was located two tenths of a mile beyond the finish of the 26-mile race. As a result, the marathon became 26.2 miles to accommodate the king.

This became the official distance, after much argument and discussion, in the 1924 Paris Olympics.

Today we have the marathon race, which is named after the herb fennel and whose distance was determined by the British King's reviewing stand location.

A Chronicle of My Running Past

Running for me as I grew up, included the distance around the bases in baseball or the length of the football field that I cut out of the woods on an old potato garden from years ago on my parents' property in Cable, Wisconsin.

While I was a junior at Cable High School, the last year of the 52-student high school's existence, I wanted to play in the intramural basketball tournament despite a high fever. I did. We juniors won over the seniors. I stuffed Billy Reser going up for a shot, something special for someone 5'6". I went outside after a shower in typical March weather and my dad ended up taking me to the doctor. I fainted in the waiting room and later learned I had spinal meningitis. After I spent several days in the hospital, the doctor told me running probably wouldn't be part of my life anymore. His warning didn't stop me. I picked up on cross-country skiing and did the American Birkebeiner several times.

The American Birkebeiner is a fifty-kilometer (31-mile) cross-country ski race. The course cuts a trail as wide as a highway through the forest of Northwest Wisconsin, between Cable, population 800 (with surrounding area), and Hayward, population 2,300. It is one of the toughest courses in the world. After two kilometers of fairly flat terrain, the hills start. They gain four hundred feet in elevation by kilometer thirteen and continue to about kilometer 47 and Lake Hayward, which leads to Main Street Hayward where thousands of spectators line the snow-covered street cheering the finishers on to the finish line. Competitors range from recreational skiers to Olympians.

The race started in 1973 with 34 competitors and has grown to about ten thousand racers today. I started skiing the race in 1977 at age 24 and haven't missed a race since. I decided if I could ski, I could run. So while working on my master's degree in 1982 at

Colorado College in Colorado Springs, Colorado, I heard about a five-mile running race on a path along Fountain Creek. Dressed in jeans and $19.95 Payless sneakers, I ran the race, finishing in the middle of the pack.

I forgot about running for a couple of years and got married in 1984. Denise and I moved to the plains of eastern Colorado in the town of Burlington, where tumbleweed still gets caught in the telephone wires. I taught in the neighboring town of Cheyenne Wells, forty miles away.

Our Eastern Colorado tumbleweed Christmas tree

Bored after school, I tried running again. First I made it around the school. I increased my distance little by little over time, to 12 miles. I took Buford, my Cocker Spaniel, with me. I became good at standing off unfriendly dogs or we'd be in tough shape.

Two years on the western plains was enough so we bought a log home in the middle of eighteen acres outside my hometown of Cable, Wisconsin. It took a little determination and time, but I eventually found a teaching position in the area.

In 1987 a group of guys, myself included, decided to put Grandma's Marathon in Duluth, Minnesota on our "bucket list." Watching the race broadcast on local television added to the incentive to take on the marathon. I tried to run a little, Ron, another one of the guys, ran dribbling a basketball, and the others played softball as training. I think we all finished in under seven hours but it wasn't real impressive, especially when my brother Bryan stopped and bought a Snickers Bar and Steve stopped and bought a beer during the race. Ron, who trained with a basketball, did the best at four hours plus. My youngest brother, Lon, and I are the ones who stuck with running. It was just a one-time lark for the others.

Grandma's Marathon was first run in 1973 with 150 runners. Today there are about 10,000 runners. The event got its name from Grandma's Restaurant, the founding sponsor, which is still involved with its location at the finish. Grandma's was founded on the legend of Rosa Brochi, who opened her first boarding house for lonely sailors in Duluth around the turn of the 20th Century and based her business on pleasing the customers. Grandma's Restaurant does the same. Grandma's continued to be the marathon I shot for each year until June of 1998, when I decided to try the Taos Marathon in Taos, New Mexico.

I also ran marathons in Utah, Montana, Iowa, and South Dakota before Denise, Lon, and I went to Alaska in August of 2003 to do Humpy's Marathon in Anchorage and to visit my aunt, cousin, and her family in Fairbanks. On the trip up to Fairbanks, we went salmon fishing on the Talkeetna River with a guide and two other fishermen. The topic came up of me doing a marathon in each state. While we cruised up the river, at a pretty good speed, one of the fishermen asked Denise if I was really serious about doing a marathon in each state at my age. I was 51. That was all it took. Since then I have been doing four marathons a year in other states. No one is going to tell me I can't do something.

This situation reminds me of another guy in our country's past. Born into a rich New York City family, he was in very poor health with asthma as a young person. This young man wasn't going to let his health keep him down. He took on a physical life with rowing, boxing, and later in life as a cowboy, hunter, and even a soldier. He set his philosophy of life in these words:

> It is not the critic who counts. The credit belongs to the man in the arena, whose face is marred by dust and sweat and blood; who strives valiantly. Who knows the great enthusiasms, the great devotions; who spends himself in a worthy cause; who at the best knows in the end the triumph of high achievement, and who at the worst, if he fails, at least fails while daring greatly.

This was our 26th President, Theodore Roosevelt who didn't live to be an old man but he lived every one of his 60 years to its fullest.

Grandma's Marathon

Duluth, Minnesota

I've completed Grandma's Marathon at least twenty times. Sometimes I've had my best times at Grandma's. Other times I have felt like the frog Mark Twain talks about in Calavaras County, loaded down with buckshot so he couldn't move. Warm, humid weather, and knees that sometimes don't work right make me feel like the buckshot-loaded frog.

The race weekend starts as a bit of a money-grab, or as Oxford Dictionary puts it, an undignified acquisition of large sums of money. You have to admit, giving a runner the choice between staying in Duluth for at least two nights at jacked-up rates, or making a second trip to pick up our registration packet with our race bib the day before the race, is a little much.

I take Thomas Jefferson seriously when he said, "Never spend your money before you earn it." I make the two trips and get up early on race day to make my second journey to Duluth to catch the 6 AM bus to the start in Two Harbors from the Duluth Convention Center parking lot.

The first seventeen miles of the course are great with rolling hills and usually cool breezes from the nearby shores of Lake Superior. Then we head down to the Lester River Bridge and on to the streets of Duluth. At about mile 22 you can see Lemon Drop Hill coming up. It isn't a huge hill, but it does have length to it, and it is the biggest hill in the marathon. We have also run 22 miles by the time we come to it. Spectators and music are loud and in abundance in the city. I prefer the quieter part of the route by the lakeshore with a little softer bagpipe music along the way.

We finish by running downtown on the brick streets and heading east over the freeway, around the lakeside of the Convention Center, and past the Irvin, a docked ore carrier. We complete the S shape that makes up the last mile of the race by heading down to Grandma's Restaurant and the finish line.

Every year my goal was for a better finish time. I seemed to get stuck around a 3 hour, 35 minute finish. Looking back now, that was an excellent time, but I had it in my head that I could get under three and a half hours.

June 19, 1993, when I was forty-one, looked like a good year. I remember the day as being cool and cloudy. About halfway through the race, it began to drizzle. The temperature dropped into the 40s. I always try to build up some reserve minutes in the first half of the race so I can back off a little in the second half. I could build up only one and a half minutes on a three-and-half-hour marathon, but it was enough. I finished in 3 hours and 29 minutes, just under an eight-minute mile. The cool, drizzly weather helped me achieve my goal. This was a proud moment.

My dad was there that day. I always wondered what he thought. He was the guy who carried one of the first electric generator-powered chainsaws through waist-deep snow up in the Bayfield area cutting timber in the mid 1950s. He prided himself in being able to hike long distances through the woods at a good pace. He didn't brag, but you knew it was important to him. Now here was his son running 26.2 miles in three and a half hours. By the way, this is the son who on my first day at Drummond High School, a teacher asked me, "Are YOU Big Donny Anderson's kid?" My dad never had much to say at the race finish other than, "Your mother is waiting in the car." I do give him credit for being there.

Taos Marathon

Taos, New Mexico

In 1998 I began thinking, " Grandma's Marathon is great but I'd like to run a marathon in another state." I chose Taos, New Mexico, in the first weekend of June. The adobe buildings and Spanish influence give the area a foreign feeling to someone from northern Wisconsin, although I was somewhat familiar with the area from my days at Colorado College in Colorado Springs.

Taos is a quiet mountain town with many artists and their galleries. Taos also includes the Pueblo Indians and the longest, continuously- lived-in pueblo village in America. It has been occupied for the last 1,000 years. I'm amazed that so much history, some violent, took place, in this adobe-built mountain community.

The Pueblo Indians are a secretive people, making tourists poking around their homes difficult to deal with, but money is money, so they put up with it. Blue Lake sits above their pueblo in the Sangre de Cristo Mountains. The Pueblo people believe Blue Lake, their place of origin, is sacred ground. They hold a pilgrimage there each year with a ceremony of bringing young people to spiritual maturity so they can be full participants in Kiva religious ceremonies.

Back in 1680, the Pueblo Indians grew sick of Spanish rule and the harsh treatment by Catholic priests. In Taos, they killed the priest and destroyed the Catholic Church. In 1847, another revolt took place, this time against the U.S. government as part of the Mexican War. The Pueblo Indians and Mexicans in the area resented the way U.S. soldiers treated them.

The insurgents also feared the loss of their land under United States control, so they attacked Governor Charles Bent of New Mexico Territory even though he had gone to the army and told them to lay off the locals. The Pueblo and Mexican rebels put two arrows in Governor Bent and scalped him, but he survived. He escaped by digging a hole through the adobe wall of his home with the help of his wife and Mrs. Kit Carson. You can still see the hole today. The insurgents caught up to and killed Governor Bent and other government officials, but left the women and children alone.

The next day the Mexican and Pueblo insurgents grew to 500. They attacked a mill outside of Taos, protected by only 10 mountain men. Eight of the men were killed in fighting during the day and two escaped under cover of darkness that night. The insurgent number grew again to 1500 and the U.S. Army moved in to stop them. The army beat back the insurgents, who took shelter in an adobe Taos church. The army moved in on the church and with the help of cannon fire, killed 150 insurgents and took 400 captives, 28 of whom were hanged in the Taos Plaza.

With this history for a backdrop, the first Saturday in June 1998 saw about 100 runners lined up at 6 AM outside the Pueblo village ready to do battle against the hills of the Taos Marathon. We were about 7,000 feet in elevation. The first half of the marathon went well with a cloudy sky and a rolling incline. Then came the mile and a half uphill. I kept reaching a plateau and then going up again. I remember passing a couple of runners on the way up. At the top, a flat stretch led to a welcome aid station and the intersection with the main highway back down into Taos. The only problem was, the sun came out to warm things up. The traffic wasn't helpful either. After passing all the billboards leading into town we turned onto residential streets. Finally we got to Kit Carson Park and the finish line.

Bruce Gomez, the community-minded race organizer, had put his touch on the race finish by having Taos Elementary School second-graders paint the clay finisher medals we all received. He also has had race proceeds passed on to help pay bills for a young Taos man with leukemia.

I finished my second state marathon in 4 hours and 13 minutes. I hung around for the awards and looked through the town plaza at some of the shops, while listening to Indian flute music performed in the town square. The music seemed to fit the place and time. It was pretty special to be there at a peaceful time, especially considering the violence of times past.

Northern Wisconsin Marathons

Paavo Nurmi 1998 Hurley, WI

Whistlestop 1998, 1999 Ashland, WI

American Birkebeiner 2012 Cable, WI

I have completed three different marathons in Wisconsin, all of them within 40 miles of Lake Superior. As Garrison Keillor would say about the Northland, " This is the land where the women are strong, the men are good looking, and the children are above average." This is home.

The first one I ran was Paavo Nurmi, held the second week in August of 1998, one week after I had done the Firehouse Fifty, 50-mile road bike race in Grand View, WI.

My sciatic nerve was so bad at the time of the Paavo Nurmi Marathon, I had trouble walking. My concern was making it to the bus taking runners to the starting area in Upson. Getting up the steps of the bus was a challenge, but I made it. I sat by a runner from New York City with an accent that sounded Russian. He told me that in his mind, a marathon wasn't a real marathon unless you finish in less than four and one-half hours. The truth is, the average time for a male runner is 4 hours and 16 minutes and 4 hours and 41 minutes for females. The average age for the male runner is 40 and 37 for females, not to mention only one-half of one percent of Americans have ever run a marathon.

When we made it to Upson, my next goal was to hobble out of the bus and then to the start area. Once at the start line, I tried to develop a shuffle so I wouldn't hurt the sciatic too much. Somehow, I managed a pretty good pace, without hurting as much as when walking. The course ran from Upson, through Iron Belt, Montreal, and to the finish line on Silver Street in Hurley. It was a warm summer day with a high around 80 and some humidity. The racecourse's rolling hills seemed to grow in the second half of the course. The finish line looked pretty good after 4 hours and 13 minutes out on the course. I looked in the race results after the race to see if the New York City runner made it in four and one-half hours. He didn't. I wonder if his idea of a marathon changed?

Silver Street was a different place 100 years ago. In the days of "Hayward, Hurley, or Hell," Silver Street had a reputation for it's wild entertainment. Saloons, dance halls, and ladies added to the entertainment. Workers from the white pine timber industry and the iron ore mining industry fueled these businesses. In the 1930s Al Capone, John Dillinger, and Baby face Nelson were seen on the streets of Hurley. Ralph Capone, Al's brother even retired in Iron County and died in a Hurley nursing home in 1974.

Two months after the Paavo Nurmi, I was at it again and only 40 miles away. I wanted to run the inaugural Whistlestop Marathon from Iron River to Ashland. The course is almost all on the railroad grade, except for the last couple of miles through the streets of Ashland. I finished the race in 4 hours and 1 minute. The course was flat with no more than a three percent grade. It ran fairly straight with plenty of shade from bordering trees. You can pretty much depend on cool October temperatures so I was disappointed with my time. I had to come back the next year and I finished in 3 hours and 58 minutes. That change from four hours to three hours was important to me at the time.

The Whistlestop has given the railroad grade a new life, but the ore docks aren't so fortunate. Since iron ore mining ended in the Iron County area in the mid 1960s, the trains obviously aren't hauling iron ore to the docks to be loaded on the ships, so the ore docks have been torn down.

Backtracking a bit, in May of 1998 I was part of an eight-person mixed relay team in the 80-mile Woods to Water Relay Race. Each runner ran three 5-kilometer segments throughout the day, handing the team baton on to the next team runner when they finished a segment. All team members not running at the time got to ride in or drive the decorated team van. The route, both on and off road, started on Lake Owen Drive outside of Cable. It went north through Drummond, Delta, the jack pine barrens, and on to the outskirts of Washburn, partly on trails. Then the route headed to Ashland and the finish on railroad grade trails along Lake Superior.

We called ourselves "The Aging Unit," a team name that turned out to be key in our success. The race had an age handicap, so the older you are, starting at 40 years, the more minutes are subtracted from the team's final time. Andrea Carroll, Terry Tansey, Al Hoepner, and I were all in our forties, which helped the team a little. Ethel Morse and Dennis Arthur were in their fifties, helping the team a little more. Darrell Thompson, our team captain, helped the most, being in his sixties. Our team finished in 9 hours and 42 minutes but with our age handicap our time was 8 hours and 2 minutes. We won. We gave credence to Mark Twain's statement, "Age is a matter of mind over matter. If you don't mind, it doesn't matter."

The next year, our team was back but with temperatures reaching well into the 90s. Just finishing was the goal. I made it through my third leg of the race but once I handed off the baton I collapsed into a drainage ditch. I wasn't going to let the team down. I remember praying, " Lord help me get to Ethel and the baton exchange." I did it and no more. The team awarded me the "Aging Unit" team baton for my effort that year.

Abraham Lincoln made the statement; " In the end it's not the years in your life that count. It's the life in your years."

I like to think that these events represent some of the life in my years. I also think the life in your years can lead to more years of life. Look at Jack Rabbit Johannsen; he lived to be 111 (1875-1987). He is credited with bringing cross-country skiing to North America. He spoke of getting out in the outdoors, which was out in the bush of Norway during his younger days. He pointed out that hockey, football, baseball, etc. are good sports but once a young person finishes playing them in school, his physical activity often ends, leaving him with a big potbelly.

I saw Jackrabbit at the opening ceremonies of the American Birkebeiner when he was 106. He just raised his cane and it brought applause from the crowd. He was still skiing at this point in his life as I understand, but a mile is about as far as he could go. He said his balance wasn't too good anymore.

The Birkebeiner ski race has always been a special time of year for me, kind of like a second Christmas. It is great being in a race with some of the best skiers in the world, finishing in around two hours. I finish in about three and a half hours, but it is more about the personal stories of those who may take five, six, or more hours to reach Main Street and the finish line in Hayward.

I remember a skier named Elmer who was fighting cancer but wanted more than anything to finish his twentieth Birkie so he would earn his membership in the Birchleggers Club of those completing twenty-plus Birkebeiners. Elmer lost his battle to cancer before the race. His church pastor wouldn't let Elmer's dream die. He carried a backpack during the race that year with Elmer's ashes inside and his race number on the outside. Elmer literally finished his twentieth Birkie on his pastor's back.

My 20th Birkie in 1996. Above center is Elmer, who would've had his 20th in 1997. He did with his pastor's help.

It is my 37th Birkie this year. Not many skiers have done more. My brothers and I have done103 Birkebeiners between us. Lon, age 54, has done 34 and Bryan, age 56, has done 32. The KBJR TV News out of Duluth-Superior even did a lead story on us when we hit one hundred Birkies among the three of us.

In 2012   the Birkebeiner   offered a Warrior Series Award.   It included doing the Birkebeiner tour, ski race, and marathon. Knowing and respecting the Birkebeiner ski race, I had thought a trail marathon on those continuous steep hills was a little much. I went out and broke the trail into segments and saw how long it would take me to run each segment. I had entered the race and was feeling that five hours was doable. That Warrior jacket was hanging out there as a "carrot."

Saturday, September 21st of 2012 was a cool day. Even a little snow covered the trail in protected areas. With sun shining for the 8 AM start of the Birkebeiner Marathon at Fish Hatchery outside of Hayward, 117 runners lined up at the start line. I began letting it roll on the down hills and using little steps on the up hills. I used this system all the way to Highway OO, the halfway point, without walking up any of the hills, in 2 hours and 15 minutes. I started thinking if I don't start walking some of the steeper up hills, the end of the race won't be pretty. Familiarity with the course from running all parts, not to mention skiing the whole course 35 times didn't hurt in planning my attack.

Once I reached the high point with about 13 kilometers to go, the down hills became more frequent. When I crossed Timber Trail Road, the trail became more rolling with four and one-half miles to the finish. The trail trekkers showed up quite often at this point and we had to maneuver around them. Half-marathoners were fresh and seemed to zip by. I finished feeling fairly strong in 4 hours and 40 minutes. I was 52nd out of 117 finishers, not bad for a 60-year-old. I received my Warrior jacket and a hot beef sandwich. It was a good day.

The Great Salt Lake and Brigham Young's
Salt Lake City home

The Salt Lake City Deseret News Marathon

Salt Lake City, Utah

I must start the story of this marathon with the history behind it, at least part of it. The Mormons are a hardworking, dedicated group of people who honor their Church of the Latter Day Saints. The problem is, they have had a way of bringing on anti-Mormon feelings in many of the places they settled. In Missouri, armed conflict broke out between the state militia and the Mormons. They moved to a swampy area in Illinois in 1839 and their settlement of Nauvoo grew to almost the size of Chicago. Joseph Smith, the Latter Day Saints founder and leader said, he had a revelation that plural marriages were a good thing. He took the revelation seriously by having 25 wives. His successor, Brigham Young, had 55 wives and 57 children. I understand there were also 23 divorces. That speaks to me of overdoing something, but there is a lot I don't understand.

Joseph Smith continued to alienate himself and his people by preaching that those who follow God's laws can become gods. Then he ordered a newspaper company destroyed because it didn't agree with him. Smith was put under arrest for his actions. He and his brother Hyram were killed by a mob in June of 1844.

In February of 1847, the Mormon people decided to go in different directions. Some stayed in Nauvoo, some traveled east, and others made an exodus to the west under the leadership of Brigham Young. Winter travel was difficult for this westward exodus, so they stopped at the Missouri River near present day Omaha, Nebraska, until the end of April. Then the Mormon exodus continued west, looking for a new homeland outside United States territory.

The Wasatch Mountains had not been crossed many times, so Brigham Young looked for the best route. The Donner Party had gone over the Wasatch the year before and did considerable work making the route passable. The Mormon expedition chose this route. It is the same route as the Deseret Marathon takes. The Mormon advance party made it down to the valley and two days later, July 24th, 1847, Brigham Young made it to the valley in the back of a wagon. Ill with Rocky Mountain Fever, he declared that this would be the Mormon Promised Land.

The Mormon trek over the mountains was the basis for Pioneer Days and the Deseret Marathon. Denise and I flew over the route of the whole exodus in a couple of hours before landing in Salt Lake City.

Saturday morning, July 24th of 2001, began early. I had to be at the University of Utah's Rice Stadium at 3:45 AM to catch a bus ride to the start of the race at Dell Golf Course in the mountains. The course is obviously named after Dell Mountain, where many Mormon pioneers camped out before making their descent to the Salt Lake Valley. I remember looking for a place in the dark to stay warm while waiting for the 5 AM start.

The first hour of the race took place in the dark and included a six mile out and back. I worried about stepping on another runner's shoes. There were 639 of us. We started at 5,880 feet and worked our way up to 6,227 feet on Little Mountain before letting it roll down Emigration Canyon. It started heating up as we reached the Salt Lake Valley and the streets of Salt Lake City. It was probably between 40 and 50 degrees at the start, 80 degrees was a pretty sure bet at the finish, with 90 degrees later in the day.

I understand it took the Mormon pioneers and their wagons four days to make this trek. It took me 4 hours and 21 minutes. Those last miles through the streets of Salt Lake City, toward Liberty Park, as the temperatures rose, were the hardest at an elevation of 4,265 feet. The finish of the marathon kind of introduced the Pioneer Day Parade. I was the 393rd finisher. This is the oldest marathon west of the Rocky Mountains, starting in 1970.

Denise and I visited the Mormon Tabernacle and Brigham Young's Beehive home while we were in the area. Each of Brigham Young's wives had her own space and abided by a sort of family government to keep peace. We also went to the salt flats and the Great Salt Lake. The lake is so shallow, you can walk about a mile out and only be waist deep. Brine flies are everywhere along with an unpleasant salty smell, but you can definitely float.

Brigham Young made the statement, "Never let a day pass that you will have cause to say, I will do better tomorrow." Good advice.

Governor's Cup Marathon

Helena, Montana

May 31 of 2002, Lon and I put our kayaks in at the Musselshell River during a side trip. The river runs entirely in Montana. It looked peaceful enough, but it had several surprises. Most of the land bordering the river is privately owned so there aren't many access points. The river received its name from Lewis and Clark, who saw the freshwater mussels in the river and gave it the name Musselshell.

The last wild buffalo herd was in the Musselshell area. In 1886, William Temple Hornaday came out to this area, sent by the Smithsonian Institute, to harvest a number of buffalo, while a few remained, for their museum. The question I have is, why kill the few wild buffalo left when there was still a chance to save them? I guess Hornaday figured he would bring a few back to Washington D.C. so everyone could see what wild buffalo looked like before someone decided to kill the remaining ones for their own use. Still, 25 buffalo seems like overkill. Today a lot of the Musselshell's water is used for irrigation on farms and ranches. Parts of the river dry up, or almost, in late summer and fall because of irrigation. The river does get its revenge in the spring sometimes. In May of 2011, Roundup, Montana, was flooded twice in two weeks by the Musselshell. The Rosy Bee Restaurant, where we ate on our way through, had water well up on the front windows during the flooding.

It was Rocky Mountain spring runoff season when we kayaked down the river. The current was fast and tricky. Water also flowed right over the banks on meanders. Ranchers had at least 10 fences across the river, marking land. That, along with several downed cottonwoods, made our portages a challenge and a lot of work. Lon brought his fishing pole along because few fishermen get on the river. He lost the pole and got wet besides, when he turned over on a hairpin turn with the changing current.

We came across a sheep ranch and asked a young fellow where we were and how far to the next landing. He talked to us as if surprised to see anyone on the river. We finally pulled out at a dirt road and walked to the highway. A guy from the area in a pickup stopped and gave us a ride back to our pickups, about four miles away. We loaded our kayaks and headed into Helena for the marathon pasta dinner.

The next morning, we boarded a bus at 5:15, which took us to the old mining town of Marysville. One of Montana's leading gold producers, 4,000 people lived there in the 1890s. Today there are 80 residents, mostly commuters to Helena for work. In the 1880s and 90s there were several grocery stores, tailor shops, jewelry stores, dry-good stores, a lumberyard, a dozen saloons, three churches, and a school with 250 students. Today most of Marysville's buildings have the doors and windows knocked out. A cemetery dates back to the 1890s.

The race started here at 7 AM. We headed out of town on a dirt road for about 6 miles. The road started at 5,400 feet and had a downhill grade to it, which was a good thing. Along the road there was more dirt, a little sagebrush, and a tuft of other vegetation here and there. One lady runner decided she had to take a wiz. Privacy being a problem, she decided to pull off the road and do what she had to do. This wouldn't have been a big deal, but she came back and caught up to the guy she was running with and discussed with him for the next several miles why she did what she did in a very audible voice. Let it go, lady!

We finally hit pavement for a while before an out and back on another dirt road over a railroad track. A wind showed up here, which is helpful only one way. Back on the pavement, four miles of huge hills faced us. They just sat out there for us to stare at. Finally I got across them and headed down into the valley and the streets of Helena at 4,200 feet. I finished in 4 hours and 20 minutes. Lon finished in 4 hours and 11 minutes. He was 94th and I was 114th out of 222 finishers.

Des Moines Marathon

Des Moines, Iowa

I heard that Des Moines, Iowa, scheduled a marathon in 2002. Denise's sister and brother-in-law live there, so I decided to do their inaugural race. Denise grew up forty miles north of Des Moines in the town of Ogden. Kate Shelley became famous three miles from there in the small village of Moingona.

Kate Shelley, a seventeen-year-old in 1881, did her best to take care of the livestock on their family tenant farm. Her father had been killed in a railroad accident and her older brother drowned in the Des Moines River. She was left with her mother to take care of the farm.

Thunderstorms began hitting one July evening and flash floods were a danger. She had to move the livestock to high ground. Between the flashes of lightning and crashes of thunder, she heard a bang and sizzle down by the river. The Honey Creek Bridge and a train with four men on board went down in the river. Kate saw two of the men hanging on to branches and told them she was going for help. She made her way across the Des Moines River Bridge with her father's lantern, the flame went out in the wind. The bridge wasn't made for pedestrians. Boards had been taken out of the base so people wouldn't try walking across the bridge, 184 feet above the river. Kate crawled across on the rails with lightning her only light, rail spikes ripping her clothes, and a wild river roaring below. Somehow she made it to the station at Moingona. She fainted when she got there but came to in time to tell the agent about the train in the river, four men needing help, and most important, to stop the oncoming passenger train. The two men hanging on to tree branches from the train crash were saved. Another man's body was later found in a cornfield, and the last one was never found. The passengers on the train Kate helped stop gave her $200. The railroad gave her another $100 as well as a half-barrel of flour, a half load of coal, and a gold watch. She became world famous for her deed, and immortalized in songs written about her.

A marathon is another kind of challenge. Gary, our brother-in-law, took me to the start while the rest of the family went to church. The gun went off at 7 AM. After five miles through the city, we reached the gold domed state capital. We continued through the city, making several turns at city street intersections. The whole state is set up much like a giant checkerboard. Highways run in straight lines with soybean and cornfields on the sides. There are small towns at or near most intersections. On any night you can go outside and look in any direction and see the lights of the next small town. Each town has a café where the farmers and other locals meet for coffee to discuss the weather, which is the lifeblood of the farming industry. Local sports are the other topic of discussion, as baseball, football, basketball, and softball are the entertainment for Iowans. Everyone plays or watches the games. It's pretty much a fulltime occupation for grandparents. There are no pro teams, but college sports are huge. Iowa girl's basketball had a unique feature until recently. Formerly there were six girls on a team, three on defense, three were on offense, and no one crosses the centerline. Denise was all state on defense in high school.

Now back to the marathon. The first half of the marathon featured some fair-sized hills with complainers to describe every feature in them. Mile 10 took us by Drake University. At this point we went through a series of parks; Greenwood, Water Works, and Gray Lake. Parts of this section of the race were run on Bill Riley Trail and downhill portions were more noticeable.

Bill Riley helped make famous another Iowa institution, the State Fair. One million people attend each year. Not bad for a state of three million. A novel and three movies have been made about the fair. It is also listed as one of the thousand places to visit before you die. There are 600 exhibitors, 60 foods on a stick, and a five and one-half foot by eight-foot cow sculptured out of butter. All of this along with the Bill Riley talent show which culminates from 100 talent shows around the state. He ended up in the Rock-n-Roll hall of fame for his efforts.

Court Street is coming up and there is the finish line. I made it in 4 hours and 10 minutes. That was good for 522nd out of 1028 finishers. Today the race has grown to 8,500 runners, but I'm sure that includes all events. Church being let out, Gary came to take me to his place for Sunday dinner Iowa style, before we headed back north to Cable.

Deadwood Mickelson Trail Marathon

Deadwood, South Dakota

On June 7th, 2003, Lon and I found ourselves in the heart of Lakota Sioux sacred country, otherwise known as the Black Hills. We stayed at Deadwood, which in my mind, is the center of the Wild West. That Friday night we ate at a casino. I don't remember if it was the casino or the motel, but one of them gave each of us a chip to play in the casino machines. It burned a hole in Lon's pocket, but he never did get to spend it.

After supper we went to the Saloon #10 and watched a reenactment of Wild Bill Hickok sitting at a card game with his back to the door, something he normally would never have done. Jack McCall came in and shot him in the back while Wild Bill held the famous "dead man's hand." Jack McCall was caught and claimed that he was getting revenge for his brother's death. A trial was reenacted in a nearby building and Lon was on the jury. Jack McCall was set free and Bill Hickok was buried in Mount Mariah Cemetery. Wild Bill Hickok lived by violence and died by violence. Calamity Jane, Wild Bill's Deadwood carousing partner, was later buried next to him.

The next morning Lon and I got on the bus for the 23-mile ride into the Black Hills for the 7 AM start of the Deadwood Michelson Trail Marathon at the ghost town of Rochford, South Dakota. Rochford consists of a Methodist Church, where the race starts, Moonshine Gulch Saloon, and a population of 25. Rochford got its start in 1878 when gold was found and the Montezuma Gold Mine was established. The town reached a population of 500 with six stores, three saloons, a doctor, and a church, but no cemetery because no one died there until a guy was accidentally shot in 1904. By 1880 the town was already on the decline.

The temperature on marathon day was around freezing at the start of the race, but the sun shone as 200 plus of us took off with a one-mile downhill through town before turning around and heading up the crushed rock Mickelson Trail. We gained 1,000 feet over the first half of the race. At the top, about mile fourteen, there was snow along the trail with aspen forests, rock outcroppings, and streams running through fields. We made our way down from the high point in the second half of the marathon. There was mud in this section and at one point, sliding down in the mud on a steep hill seemed the best way to go. Calamity Jane showed up about three miles outside of Deadwood, cracking her whip to spur us on. Then we came to the streets of Deadwood and the finish line where Wild Bill Hickok and Jerry Dunn, the race founder and organizer, congratulated us. I finished in 4 hours and 26 minutes, good for 105th out of 224 finishers. Lon finished in 4 hours and 2 minutes. He was 57th.

The next day I decided to ride my Stump Jumper mountain bike on the last 83 miles of the Mickelson Trail. Lon went fishing. I left Rochford heading south. The terrain changed in time, from mountains and Ponderosa Pine to open range and farm land. Before I left the mountains I could see the Crazy Horse Monument. Farther south stood a big sawmill in the town of Pringle and before I reached Edgemont and the end of the trail, I came to a large gorge with a railroad bridge over it. When the bridge was used for trains and not bikes, the engineers did not always trust the bridge so they stopped the train just before the bridge and one engineer hiked across the bridge while the other engineer put the train in gear and hopped off the train. The train made its way across the bridge on its own. The engineer on the other side stopped the train and waited for the first engineer to make his way across the bridge before they completed their journey. I completed my journey at Edgemont before backtracking on my Stump Jumper to Custer to get my pickup. It was definitely time to go home.

Wild Bill Hickok and Calamity Jane's final resting place in Deadwood's Mt. Moriah Cemetery

Humpy's Marathon

Anchorage, Alaska

In Mid August of 2003, Denise, Lon, and I flew into Anchorage, Alaska. Humpy's Marathon summoned us, but we had some other plans first. We drove south and compared some of Alaska's glaciers to those we'd seen in Glacier National Park. Exit Glacier is huge in comparison, but shrinking, as markers leading to it attest. From there we headed north to the Talkeetna River to try salmon fishing, with little luck, but this is where Denise discussed me finishing a marathon in each state and another fisherman thought I was a little old to try such a thing.

Denali National Park was our next stop, but we had to settle for a bus tour. One day each September is the only day cars are allowed to roam the park. We did see Mt.McKinley a long way off, along with wildlife all over, including bear, reindeer, and wolves. That evening we went river rafting, Denise's favorite activity. I usually have red marks on my arm where she has been hanging on.

The next day in Fairbanks we met my Aunt Eileen Houger at a gas station in her full-sized 1985 Cadillac. Aunt Eileen is a true Alaskan pioneer despite her Cadillac.

My Uncle Beryl and Aunt Eileen moved to Alaska in 1954 from Pettibone, North Dakota. Neither of them knew what to expect, since they nor their two small children, Weldyn and Charlene, had ever been there before. The family took up residence in Elim, Alaska, where my uncle taught school. Elim is a small village not far from Nome on the Bering Sea. People there traveled by dog sled and a plane occasionally landed on the beach. The Houger family didn't leave the village the whole year they were there.

Uncle Beryl and Aunt Eileen made Alaska their home. They did make one trip back to North Dakota to pick up some belongings in a trailer pulled by their Willys car. On their way back to Alaska, on the then primitive dirt Alaskan Highway, they ran into flooding that washed some of the highway away in torrents of water. They even saw a new Hudson automobile that had been abandoned after being washed away. The path of the road was actually hard to find in places, but they made it. They were going to the Fairbanks area, where Uncle Beryl continued to teach. My aunt and uncle filled out papers to homestead 160 acres.

Their new log home didn't spring up overnight. They had to live in a Quonset hut while their home was being built. The Quonset was a half circle structure with insulation between two layers of canvas and logs around the bottom to help keep out the cold. One time while the family was away, a bear made itself at home and ransacked the place. When they did get their log home built, a chimney fire took it down and sent them back to the Quonset until it was rebuilt. In 1959 electric service came through, making things easier.

The agreement to homestead wasn't just for free land. Uncle Beryl and family had to clear land and plant some land in crops, along with building their home. He had a John Deere 440 Crawler to help with the work and the whole family pitched in. They raised peas, oats, and Kentucky Blue Grass. The family's Angus bull and cow grazed on their land and were joined by moose, geese, and sandhill cranes.. The cranes became so numerous they had to use scare bombs to get rid of them.

My cousin Beverly remembers hearing something outside her single-paned window when she was 10. There, a big old bear stared at her when she opened the curtains. She ran to her dad and he got out the gun. That was the end of the bear.

Indoor plumbing was another issue. They didn't have any. For bathing they had a galvanized tub hanging on the wall. Only three inches of water was allowed in the tub because water had to be carried five gallons at a time.

We stayed with Beverly, her husband Mark, and their three kids in their very modern home when we were there. We went gold mining tourist style and every one of us came away with $10 of gold that we panned. We drove by the famous Alaskan pipeline and watched a couple of musk ox in a penned area. That evening we ate at the Pump House Restaurant on the Chena River in Fairbanks. I tried reindeer stew. It was pretty good.

The next day we headed south, back to Anchorage for Humpy's Marathon. Saturday, August 17th, was cloudy, misty, and cool, probably in the mid 50s. The course was flat with only a few inclines. Of its three loops, the first took us through residential areas of the city, the second worked its way out to the earthquake area, and the third went along Cook Inlet. The race was all on bike trails. I finished in 3 hours and 58 minutes, which was good for 56th overall and fifth in my age class. Lon finished in 3 hours and 41 minutes and was 32nd overall. He was seventh in his age class, so that proves getting older has its advantages. He is eight years younger than I. There were 232 finishers in all. It was time to fly home.

Cruising up the Talkeetna River looking for salmon with the fisherman who thought I was too old to run a marathon in every state.

Aunt Eileen's family homestead and their Quonset in the inset

Denise watches as Aunt Eileen pans for gold.

Ozark Mountain Marathon

Branson, Missouri

On November 21of 2003, Denise and I made our way south toward Branson, Missouri. The next day we met Denise's sister Deb and brother-in-law Gary in very mild Branson. It was in the 70s. We went to a musical comedy that Saturday evening. The music was good, but the comedy was even better. Laughter flew all over that room.

Sunday morning November 23rd started out in the 60s, but it changed fast. The temperature dropped to the 40s as Gary drove me the 20 or so miles north to Ozark, Missouri, the start area of the marathon and ultramarathon. The wind and rain moved in by the time we made it to Lambert's Café where we waited for the 7 AM start. Water was pouring off the roof of the café. At the start, I wore a Patagonia fleece jacket that I keep with me to stay warm in weather like this.

The race consisted of a few ultramarathoners and eight marathoners, including myself. At the beginning of the race we wound through a side road before heading out to the shoulder of Interstate 65 in a head wind to cross wind and, of course, rain. This race was advertised as one of the toughest marathons in America, and now we had wind and rain to add to it. The oncoming Interstate traffic was an ongoing issue, although it was light at the beginning because it was Sunday morning. The second half of the race was the real kicker, although the rain let up. We ran five huge hills, one mile up, one mile down, five times. These weren't mere inclines, these were hills.

When I reached the mark of the marathon finish, I was told a mistake had been made and I had to climb one more hill to make it to the actual finish line. That statement just didn't hit me right, especially after the rain, wind, huge hills, and now numbing cold.

I did make it to the finish line. There was a van waiting to take finishers back to Branson. There weren't many around so visions of grandeur went through my mind. There were only eight marathoners. Maybe I won? That wasn't to be, but I did win my age class, such as it was, in a time of 4 hours and 9 minutes, which made me plenty proud. As an age class winner I received a piece of rock with a base mount. The rock had been blasted from the hills along the route when they built the freeway. It was a different sort of event, but memorable in its own way and my 9th state marathon was complete.

The camera doesn't do justice to those mile-long hills in the second half of the Ozark Mt. Marathon. I'm one cold, wet finisher in the top picture..

Country Music Marathon

Nashville, Tennessee

In the spring of 2004, Denise and I headed south for Tennessee. We drove to Memphis before working our way toward Nashville and yet another marathon. We talked about stopping at Graceland, just outside of Memphis, but we decided $25 per person, was a bit much. So we passed Elvis's luxury home, 33 cars, and personal jet.

One hundred miles down the road, we found Shiloh Battlefield. It is free. This is the battle where the Confederacy under General Sidney Johnston took the offensive and surprised the Union Army under General Grant. If it wasn't for Major General William Wallace's men spotting the Southern activity and holding them off for most of April 6th, 1862 with a force of about 5,700 men in what was called the "Hornet's Nest," the Union may have lost the battle. As it was, Wallace gave General Grant enough time to get his army in place before Confederate General Ruggles moved in 62 cannons and blew Wallace out of his position. At about this time, Confederate Commander Sidney Johnston found himself in a bad place. He was wounded in the back of the knee and bled into his boot. No one knew anything was wrong until he became so weak, he fell off his horse, and died.

The next day with Grant in position, the South was in some disarray. The Union Army pushed the South back in fierce fighting until they had to take the road back to Corinth, Mississippi and regroup. There were 23,746 casualties at Shiloh, more than any previous Civil War Battle. Regretfully, it would only stand a couple months as a record. It struck me that 600,000 visitors come to Elvis Presley's home each year and only 300,000 visit Shiloh Battlefield. When the choice is history or entertainment, Americans seem more interested in entertainment. Mark Twain once said, "Whenever you find yourself on the side of the majority, it is time to pause and reflect." Denise and I obviously didn't have that problem of being on the side of the majority. The Civil War continued to make its presence known when we got to Nashville, with the bullet hole in the wall at Bell Meade Plantation and the Battle of Stone River, not to mention the Battle of Nashville. At Stone River I asked a park ranger if the Civil War is still an issue in many Southerners minds. He diplomatically said, "yes."

On Friday, April 23rd, we got to do one of my favorite things, wait in line. I'm sure all 16,000 runners showed up at the marathon expo at the same time to get their race bibs.

Saturday morning when I got to Centennial Park for the start, the sky looked ominous. It started to rain and I tried staying under a tree until a thunderstorm broke out and we were all told to head for shelter. That is a little hard to do with 16,000 runners. Many of us stood in a carport. The 7 AM start was not going to happen. The race may have been cancelled, but the lightning let up and the officials had us lineup for a 7:30 start, in the rain. It was a crowded start with a couple of long out and backs through the city. Some of the bands were out there even in the rain. There was supposed to be a band every mile. The music I remember most was the Belmont Praise Team. They had high-energy and high-volume as the talented group belted out their music on the steps of their church. Their music echoed along the street and between the buildings as we ran by. Nashville surely lived up to its name as Music City. I heard some people complain about the hills in the race but the only hill that stood out in my mind was a series of stairs we had to climb.

The second half of the course featured warmer, then hot temperatures, with high humidity as the rain and clouds disappeared. There was the "sweet aroma" of a fertilizer plant and at mile 19 you could see the finish area, but we still had an out and back of 7 miles to go. Running in soggy shoes and sweating was causing matching misery. They said that the temperature was 75 at the finish, but I saw a bank thermometer that said 90 that afternoon. Who do you believe, the bank or public relations? It felt at least 90. I finished in 4 hours and 21 minutes. I was 1553rd out of 4073 marathon finishers.

That evening we attended the Brad Paisley and Carol Dawn Johnson concert, which was connected with the marathon. All entrants received one free ticket. We sat halfway back in the auditorium and still I plugged my ears with tissue to tone the sound down. We liked the music, just not that loud. The next day we went to an arboretum, in Nashville, which hosted a Beethoven recital. Denise and I sat in on it. In less than twenty-four hours we went from country to classical music, and I finished my tenth state marathon, all in Nashville. It was time to go home, and we did.

Sunburst Marathon

South Bend, Indiana

Saturday, June 5 of 2004, Denise and I were in South Bend, Indiana, trying to find the College Football Hall of Fame, which was the start area of the Sunburst Marathon. Once we arrived there, I had plenty of time to look at the football museum. This was definitely going to be a football-oriented marathon, starting at the hall of fame and ending outside Notre Dame Stadium. We were supposed to finish on the 50-yard line but work on the stadium made it impossible.

The race started at 5:45 AM with a sunny cool start and temperatures in the 50s. We ran through the streets of South Bend on our way to an out and back, heading north along the St. Joseph River. Once we made it back into South Bend at about mile eight, we headed southeast along the St. Joseph River for another out and back that took us to within a couple of miles of the finish. This section followed a bike path lined with trees for shade. The last couple of miles led us along the streets and even sidewalks of South Bend, taking us to Notre Dame. We encountered some rolling hills, but not bad. The biggest hill was at the end of mile 24. The aid stations were great and frequent. The finish line was below a mosaic of Jesus at a Notre Dame Library, across from the stadium. We enjoyed Popsicles at the finish. They went well with the much warmer temperatures than the start, probably 70s. I finished in 4 hours and 4 minutes. That was good for 223rd out of 416 marathon finishers. My 11th state marathon was in the bank.

Indiana is known for its Amish population. After the race Denise and I decided to visit Amish Acres and taste Amish life first hand. The Amish have their roots back in Switzerland, where they established a simple, God-fearing, family-oriented lifestyle. Many of the Amish immigrated to America. They established themselves in Northern Indiana in the 1870s. They still hold to their simple, family-oriented lifestyle, which means living without modern conveniences, including, automobiles and electricity.

We climbed onto a tractor-drawn wagon and took a tour of the Amish village. When we came to the small school, our guide pointed out how "effective" Amish education is compared to the public school.

Being an elementary teacher, I felt the hair rise on the back of my neck. I thought, if we had the control they did in the classroom, the results might be a little different in public schools. Their lifestyle is definitely an attraction for modern America and they offer some good advice for us:

Christ is the head of man, and man is the head of woman. One of the greatest needs of our time is men who will assume the responsibility God has placed on their shoulders. Not to accept that responsibility is to lie down on the job, to fail God's will.

Those are pretty strong words. One thing is for sure; they set a great table so we can have the strength to take on God's will.

DINNER
Broasted Country Chicken

Honey-baked hickory smoked Ham

Iron kettle of thick ham and bean soup

Basket of Amish Acres freshly baked hearth bread

Churned butter

Crock of locally made apple butter

Garden relish

Sweet and sour cabbage slaw

Green beans with side meat

Beef and egg noodles

Mashed potatoes and giblet gravy

Sage dressing

Choice of fruit pie

Something to drink

After this feast and a good night's sleep, Denise and I headed home.

Mesa Falls Marathon

Ashton, Idaho

In August of 2004 Denise and I drove out to the Rocky Mountains. It was cold and snowy in Jackson, Wyoming. We ate breakfast at Jedediah Smith's home, known as Jedediah's Original House of Sourdough.

Jedediah Smith survived three massacres and a bear mauling in his 32 years. He was a trapper, explorer, and cartographer who went a long way toward making the Louisiana Purchase accessible to US settlers in the 1820s and beyond. He was the first to cross the Sierra Nevadas to the Pacific Ocean. The Mexicans in California and the British in Oregon saw Smith as an American intruder. He had to work around these foreign powers, sometimes with diplomacy and sometimes with force.

Jedediah and two friends started the Rocky Mountain Fur Company, in which they did very well. When Jedediah was a part of a fur trader rendezvous, he stood out. He was the rare trapper who carried a Bible, didn't drink, didn't smoke, and didn't use profanity. The only reason he had long hair was to cover his missing ear from a bear mauling.

At 31 he decided it was time for a change, so he sold his share of the fur company and moved to St. Louis. He became involved in a supply trade company. He led a supply wagon train through southwest Kansas, then left the supply wagons to scout for water. He never returned. It was determined that some Comanches surrounded him and killed him.

We did a little hiking in the Tetons, saw a moose, and headed north toward Yellowstone. Jedediah would have been proud of us. We saw plenty of buffalo as we headed toward Old Faithful. A celebration of Christmas in August was in full swing at the Old Faithful Lodge, with tree decorating, Christmas music, cookies and punch, and Santa making his way down from the balconies of the upper floors of the lodge. It was even snowing outside! The celebration is said to have started around the turn of the 20th Century when a stagecoach full of visitors got stranded in Yellowstone during a summer snowstorm. The visitors and park workers decided to have a Christmas Party and the tradition continued. We watched the celebration with some folks from Louisiana, who thought I was fortunate that I could still run.

Friday morning, August 27th, I climbed Mt. Washburn in northwest Yellowstone. Mount Washburn is named after Henry Washburn, who led an exploration expedition in this area in 1870. The six and one-half mile round-trip took me up the mountain where I heard elk bugling. Then I saw them. It is amazing how they can fold back their huge antlers, crash through a forest with thick underbrush, and not get caught. A little later I could see some other critters coming at me. It was a little spooky being on a mountain in the fog with something foreign and puzzling coming toward me. It turned out to be several big horn sheep, who didn't exactly move over when I met them on the trail. As I gained elevation I came to snow and the fog began to clear. I finally made it up to the observation deck, where I talked to the ranger for a little while. You get quite a view from up there with the snow on the upper elevations and green down below. I didn't see any other people until I almost reached the bottom.

Later that day we drove to Ashton, Idaho for a pasta dinner at the school for those in the marathon. Ashton appears to be a typical agricultural community of 1,100 people. It claims to be the seed potato capital of the world. They definitely know how to put on a sporting event. They made all of us marathoners feel pretty special.

In the wintertime Ashton hosts the All-American Dog Sled Race, the oldest dog sled race in the United States. This February was its 90th year. It runs from Ashton to Yellowstone and back. There are five races from 7.5 miles to 92 miles. Ashton nearly always gets a pretty steady snow cover. The race started in 1917 and the only time it wasn't held was during World War II and one year when the snow was too deep for the trains to run.

On Saturday morning, August 28[th,] we had to be at the Ashton High School at 5:15 AM to get on a bus that took us to the Idaho backcountry in the Targhee Forest for the start of the Mesa Falls Marathon. It was only 37 degrees. The race started at 6:30 on a dirt road. We could see the Teton Mountains in the early morning light to the southeast and we heard the coyotes yapping to the west. Some runners saw a moose cross the road in the first mile of the race. At about mile nine we turned onto a blacktop road and at mile

11, we took a short detour to see the 65-foot Lower Mesa Falls. From there we headed off the road and onto a trail section after the half marathoners joined us. Finally we were back on the blacktop with a downhill bend to the course until we came to miles 17-20, where we did hit some uphill. We saw fields of barley as we headed down toward Ashton. The temperature rose to the 60s and it remained sunny. I finished in 3 hours and 59 minutes. That was good for 47th out of 120 marathon finishers. I had my 12th state marathon. Denise and I stayed for the awards and something to eat before we started home.

Mountain sheep coming out of the fog on Mt.Washburn with Christmas in August at Yellowstone Lodge in the inset

Independence Hall with skyscraper backdrop.
Left inset: Old Philadelphia was part of the marathon route
Right inset: After the marathon I stood in front of the art
museum made famous in the movie <u>Rocky.</u>

Philadelphia Marathon,

Philadelphia, Pennsylvania

Theodore Roosevelt, a man of action, once said, "In any moment of decision, the best thing you can do is the right thing, the next best thing is the wrong thing, and the worst thing you can do is nothing."

I kind of think Denise wishes Teddy Roosevelt would keep his thoughts to himself. On the other hand, I was out there doing my thing, right or wrong, I'm not sure. I definitely did something about the fare for a cab.

Denise and I flew into Philadelphia on Saturday, November 20, 2004. We called the Super 8 to pick us up. It was the wrong Super 8. We didn't figure that out until we were several miles from the airport. Our driver, a nice guy, said no problem, and he took us back to the airport. He also told us not to pay a cab more than $20 to get us to the historic district Super 8, our planned destination.

Denise waited behind the glass door of the airport while I called over a cab and asked how much to get us downtown. He said $25. I said no. As I recall, after some discussion, another cab driver joined the discussion. When I wouldn't give in, they called in their supervisor. Denise looked on, wondering why I was arguing over $5. The supervisor said they could only do so much and I believe we came up with a compromise. Denise came out, glad it was all over and we got our ride down to the right Super 8.

We visited the Liberty Bell that day. Today the bell is in a glass pavilion that x-ray inspection is required for entry. It is across from Independence Hall, where it had been located on the steeple until 1976. The bell was cast in London in 1752 and it cracked the first time it was rung after making it across the ocean to Philadelphia. Despite efforts to repair it, the cracks grew until it became a symbol of liberty and not a working bell, calling people to meetings. On the bell is written, Leviticus 25:10: Proclaim liberty throughout the land unto all the inhabitants thereof.

That evening we tried to take the shuttle bus for the marathon to the race packet pickup and expo. The problem was, the driver didn't speak English and didn't know where to take us. We discussed the situation with a father who worked on the tunnel under Boston Harbor, his son, and a friend who were running the marathon. We all decided to get off the bus and flag down a couple of cabs to get us to the race packet pickup. We got there just in the knick of time.

This brings me to another Teddy Roosevelt quote; "Every immigrant who comes here should be required within five years to learn English or leave the country." I think Theodore was rather lenient.

We all went to a noisy Philadelphia restaurant for burgers. Some obnoxious Iowa fans sat there watching the Wisconsin vs. Iowa football game on television. To say they were loud would be an understatement. It didn't help that Wisconsin wasn't doing well.

The next morning the television in the motel lobby gave a news flash about a Hmong hunter in Northwest Wisconsin who got ticked off at some other hunters and killed them. When something like that happens, it is shocking, and even more so when it happens in our home area. It was becoming a very eventful marathon and the race hadn't started yet.

I decided not to wait for the shuttle bus that probably wouldn't show up, so I shared a cab with three other runners to the marathon start area. For someone who had never been in a cab before, I was getting a lot of practice in one. I forgot my energy gels and that would show up in the second half of the race.

The marathon started at 8 AM with cloudy and cool weather. We made a loop through the historic district, then along streets with people cheering from row houses and businesses. We passed through some park areas, then back to the art museum to finish the first half of the race. It took me 1 hour and 54 minutes.

The second half took us along another loop in a different direction. I had little energy left without the energy gels. I remember an out and back through a park along a river from miles 18 to 24. From there we came back to the art museum and the finish. It took me 4 hours and 11 minutes. I was 3611th out of 6193 finishers and had my 13th state marathon. Denise took my picture in front of the statue by the art museum from the Rocky movie. We didn't realize it was the movie scene sight until later.

When I revived after the race, we went to old Philadelphia, which is definitely the location of the beginning of our country. It is a small area in today's world, with two-story brick buildings, which are miniaturized by skyscrapers in the background, but without the events of that small area, those skyscrapers wouldn't be what they are today. First there is Carpenter's Hall, where the first Continental Congress decided to send King George a protest letter over the Intolerable Acts in 1774. He ignored the letter, bringing on the Battles of Lexington and Concord. The colonial delegates met again in May of 1775 in Independence Hall and picked George Washington, sitting tall with his French and Indian War uniform on, bullet holes still visible, as commander of the Continental Army. This is also where, in 1776, the red-headed Thomas Jefferson had to almost be restrained by John Adams and Ben Franklin as the Congress "tore apart," in Jefferson's mind, the Declaration of Independence he had written, to make it acceptable to all present. The Constitution was put together here under the leadership of physically weak and squeaky-voiced James Madison, who had a powerful mind. Congress Hall is where George Washington's second inauguration took place and four years later turned the Presidency over to John Adams, as the rest of the world looked on in wonder at the giving up of power. George Washington told John Adams, "I am fairly out and you are fairly in, let us see which one is the happiest."

Being in those buildings with the furniture, feathered pens, and green carpeting as it was 240 years ago and knowing what went on there, is an experience every American should have.

Whiskey Row Marathon

Prescott, Arizona

On Friday, April 29 of 2005, Denise and I arrived in Prescott, Arizona, and signed in at the St. Michael's Hotel. It was built as a replacement for the burned-out Burke Hotel, lost in the 1900 fire that took out the four-and-a-half -block stretch of Prescott, Arizona, known as Whiskey Row. There were 40 saloons in that stretch of town, with gambling halls and hotels mixed in. Whiskey Row, the roughest part of town, had a 1800s row house look to it. When one building caught on fire, they all went.

The Earp brothers were known to frequent the Palace Saloon and hotel on Whiskey Row. In fact Virgil Earp lived in Prescott before and after the Tombstone years. Virgil and Allie, his common-law wife, first lived in Prescott between 1877 and 1879. Virgil and his younger brother Wyatt hauled supplies from California to Prescott. After that Virgil tried gold mining. When that didn't work too well, he ran a sawmill in the Thumb Butte area to provide timber supports for mine shafts as well as lumber to build homes. He later became town constable and was asked to come to Tombstone to help straighten out the lawlessness there.

In Tombstone, Virgil and his brothers Wyatt and Morgan were in and out of law enforcement, trying to keep the McLaury and Clantons from raising cane in town and rustling cattle out of town. Virgil was the only Earp, including Doc Holiday, who had any experience killing people. He had three years of experience in the Civil War and he killed a robber with two shots to the head in Prescott.

The outlaw cowboy problem came to a head on October 26, 1881, at the OK Corral. The three Earp brothers and Doc Holiday faced off with Ike and Billy Clanton and the other cowboys, Tom and Frank McLaury. Virgil was shot in the leg and both McLaury brothers and Billy Clanton were killed. A couple of months later, revenge was in the air and Morgan Earp was shot and killed. Virgil Earp's side and arm were filled with buckshot. His arm no longer worked. Virgil Earp and Morgan's body were taken by train to their parents' place in California. It took Virgil two years to recover. When he did, he gave mining another try in the Prescott area, only to have the mine collapse on him. Once again he was in recovery mode from an incident he should have never survived.

He and Allie tried ranching over the Weaver Mountains from Prescott near the town of Kirkland from 1898-1902. During this time, fire wiped out Whiskey Row in Prescott. It is said that customers just took their drinks across the street and watched the fire. A few more ambitious spectators carried the Brunswick Bar out of the Palace Saloon to save it.

Ranching didn't go too well for Virgil and Allie, so they started selling off their ranch land and moved to Goldfield, Nevada, where Virgil died in 1905 from pneumonia.

Whiskey Row was quickly rebuilt and the St. Michael's Hotel was a part of that rebuilding. Built of stone to resist fire, it featured gargoyles carved in the stone near the top, supposedly representing politicians. Several well-known people have stayed at the hotel including, Theodore Roosevelt, Barry Goldwater, Tom Mix, and John L. Sullivan, who I find in my family tree.

Denise and I stayed in the St. Michael's Hotel overlooking Whiskey Row. As we ate our spaghetti dinners to get a few carbs in for Saturday's marathon, we started talking with the folks at the next table. We found out their names were Jim and Diana Heinz from Las Vegas, Nevada. He had been a runner for many years and was on the same quest as I am to finish the 50 states. Jim and a couple other runners convinced me that just finishing this marathon was like a personal best. Whiskey Row Marathon is known as one of America's toughest marathons.

Saturday morning was cool, around freezing, with a clear sky. Since the start line was right outside the hotel we had no reason to hurry out except for my nervous energy, of which I have plenty. The gun went off at 7 AM and we headed down Whiskey Row where Virgil Earp patrolled the streets on foot. We came on a residential district and the hills started right there at 5,280 feet. As we ran the next nine miles, gaining elevation all the time, the houses turned into Ponderosa Pines and the blacktop turned into gravel and dirt. When we reached the high point of 7,000 feet we had a great view of the surrounding valleys. Being on Thumb Butte Road, Virgil Earp's sawmill had to be nearby. From here we headed down hill for four miles on logging roads to the half marathon turn around. A few people didn't catch the turnaround and kept going for a bit. Now it was back up to 7,000 feet in four miles with some steep winding turns before the 9-mile descent back down to Prescott. Traffic was pretty much non-existent until we got back to town.

The steep downhills were talking to my knees. Once we got out of the trees, the sun had a chance to really wear me down those last couple of miles through town. That last turn by the city park across from Whiskey Row was a wonderful sight. I finished in 4 hours and 30 minutes, good for 82nd place out of 160 finishers. I guess I answered the Whiskey Row challenge, Are you tough enough? Jim Heinz came in about 10 minutes later. Denise and I had dinner with Jim and Diana that evening and we've been doing marathons together and visiting each other ever since.

Now we have two new friends and I have my 14th state marathon.

Whiskey Row in 1890 as Virgil Earp saw it.

Whiskey Row today with the St. Michael's Hotel and the start area of the marathon at the far end of the street

I'm crossing Whiskey Row on my way to the finish with Thumb Butte Area and the high point of the race in the inset.

Estes Park Marathon

Estes Park, Colorado

In June of 2005 the Andersons took a road trip to Estes Park, Colorado. This included Lon, Bryan, and Laura with their three kids, our mother and father, and Denise and me. My dad had reached a point where traveling was very difficult because of Parkinson's disease. Oh, by the way, Lon and I were going to do the Estes Park Marathon while we were there. I rented two cabins along the Fall River, one for the guys and one for the girls. Good luck, ladies, with my mother. I wish I could get her to listen to Theodore Roosevelt's statement: "If you could kick the person in the pants responsible for most of your trouble, you wouldn't sit for a month."

My dad was no treat either, having to get up every little bit during the night, but this probably would be his last chance to travel. Steven, Bryan's oldest, made good use of the Fall River, catching one fine trout.

It was still like winter in the mountains, there was snow and water everywhere up in the High Country on the Trail Ridge Road. Snowball fights couldn't be avoided.

The day before the marathon I got the bright idea that horseback riding would be a good idea. Checking for possibilities I found this outfitter not far from the cabins who would take us horseback riding up to the high country for a steak dinner, then ride back down to the stables. They even had an answer for our mom and dad. The outfitters would load them in a big old army truck and haul them up to the high point for the steak dinner.

Later that afternoon, we loaded my mother and father on the bench in the back of the truck. We all picked out our horses and saddled up to start the trip up the mountain. My horse Lou, marched to a different drummer. He didn't necessarily want to follow the trail, didn't care if we lagged behind, and scratched himself on most available trees. One last item: I don't know what they fed the poor animal, but he kept passing gas, regularly. Denise, following me, got the full effect. She learned what is meant by don't find yourself on the south end of a north facing horse. About this time the guide got a call on his phone telling him there were two older people up at the high point who wanted to come down. Guess who they were? The guide gave the phone to my brother Bryan and he pacified our parents so they would stay put. When we reached the top, the steaks, baked potatoes, and beans looked awfully good. They looked good to my dad, too. We tried to talk him into a hamburger because there was no way he could chew a steak. He wouldn't hear of it, so he did battle with a steak the best he could.

We had quite a view of Estes Park from up there. On the way down, my horse and I seemed to get along better. I don't know if it was the horse or me that changed. Maybe going downhill made things more peaceful.

Sunday morning came around fast. After our horseback expedition and steak dinner, Lon and I had to face the highest paved marathon in the world. The sky was clear and it was quite warm for an Estes Park morning, with the temperature rising quickly. The 6 AM start was in the school parking lot at 7,550 feet. The route went through town and up to the high point at 8,150 feet at the six-mile mark. One of those hills in that section made you wonder how you would make it through the rest of the race when your legs burned from climbing the hill. From the top we worked our way back down through town to complete the first half of the race.

The second half of the race saw the temperature rise to 84 degrees as we passed through Dry Gulch and Devils Gulch on those long inclines that seemed to go on forever. The thin air allowed the heat to really penetrate so we felt the full affect. After the gulches, we headed back down into Estes Park and the school track, where you had to make it one time around to get to the finish line. Lon finished 10 minutes ahead of me, but I think he was really feeling the marathon heat and elevation. I finished in 4 hours and 41 minutes, good for 52nd out of 152 finishers. There were only 14 finishers that beat four hours. I had completed my 15th state marathon.

It was a tough day but a good day. Now we had to head down out of the mountains and on to the plains where 100-degree temperatures were a sure bet.

Our ride up to the high country
with our parents' ride in the inset

My brothers vainly try to talk my dad into a burger
instead of steak as my mother looks on.

My brother Bryan and dad watch as I finish the
world's highest paved marathon in Estes Park

Denise joins me at the pre-race dinner for the Run
with the Horses Marathon. In the background, the
high country where the first 20 miles of the race
took place. Inset: My finish on Expedition Island

Run with the Horses Marathon

Green River, Wyoming

On Friday evening, August 26 of 2005, Denise and I drove into Green River, Wyoming. I got my race packet for the Run with the Horses Marathon. The unique pasta dinner included Cajun fried shrimp and Cajun Zydeco music, in the western cowboy town. Jim Heinz was already there resting up before his second marathon in two weeks. The sun shone on a flattop mountain to the north, the site of the first twenty miles of our marathon the next morning. To the south ran the Green River, where some kayakers were testing the river.

John Wesley Powell tested the Green and Colorado Rivers in 1869, starting from the town of Green River on Expedition Island. He had four wooden boats, three heavier oak boats to carry supplies, and a lighter, faster, pine boat used to lead the way. His crew consisted of three Civil War veterans, four hunters and trappers, an English adventurer, and a cook. None of them knew what they were in for. John Wesley Powell made the statement:

We have an unknown distance yet to run, an unknown river to explore. What falls there are, we know not; what walls ride over the river, we know not. Ah well! We may conjecture many things.

They were truly exploring the last territory of the continental United States that had been left unknown.

John Wesley Powell was a college professor in Illinois, interested in geology and conservation. When the Civil War broke out, John was there to join the Union forces. At the Battle of Shiloh in 1862 he took a Confederate mini ball in the arm and had to have the arm sawed off to prevent infection. This handicap didn't deter him from his desire to search out the unknown. Constant nerve pain kept reminding him of his arm problem.

Two weeks after the explorers left Expedition Island in Green River, one of the oak supply boats got caught in a rapids called Disaster Falls and was lost with a third of their supplies. Two weeks later the English adventurer said that was enough adventure and left the expedition. The crew tried to use ropes and pull the boats around the worst of the rapids from that point on. Within two days of the canyon exit, the three hunter/trappers (two of them Howland brothers) left the expedition. They didn't know at the time they were only two days from the finish. They were never heard from again. It is believed that some Paiute Indians killed them, thinking the men were responsible for the death of an Indian woman. On August 30th, two days later, Powell, the three Civil War veterans, the 19-year-old Scottish trapper, and the cook left the canyon, completing the three-month expedition.

On Saturday morning, August 27th, 5:15 AM I had a different reason to be at Expedition Island. All marathoners had to catch a school bus to take us to the top of White Mountain and the 6 AM race start. The sun was just starting to light up the surroundings on the tabletop mountain. The colors in the sky and the shadows of distant peaks were impressive.

I probably took off too quickly, because my nose started bleeding heavily, prompting me to run with my head tilted back. Then my feet started hurting big time from my new shoes, so I had to stop and retie them. This was not a good start for the first six miles that rose 600 feet to an elevation of 7,500 feet. The temperature at the start of the race was in the upper 40s and rose to the 70s as the sun's intensity quickly heated the thin air. The dry air just evaporated the perspiration. Only one runner passed me in the whole race. A cowboy in a dirty white pickup pulled alongside of me and said he thought I was the lead runner. I wasn't. At another point I was talking to Joe, another runner, when we decided there were just rabbits up here, not horses. The food stations were different also. Everything was set out and runners had to pick up whatever they wanted. Many of the stations were placed down in the ditch.

The last six miles of the race were downhill off the mountain and back to the paved streets of Green River. My legs were talking to me on the long downhill and then we had to climb a metal staircase over a bridge that spanned the railroad yard and down the stairs on the other side. Expedition Island and the finish line were only a half-mile away. One long straight stretch and a corner brought me to the finish in 4 hours and 13 minutes. That was good for 11th place out of 57 finishers. I had completed my 16th state marathon.

Atlanta Marathon

Atlanta, Georgia

In November of 2005 Denise and I flew into Atlanta a couple of days before the Thanksgiving Day Marathon. Two of the places we visited were Plains, Georgia and the site of the Andersonville Prison Camp. Only 25 miles separate these places, but they are worlds apart in what they represent.

Plains, Georgia, population 776, is Jimmy Carter. Every place you go in that town has a Jimmy Carter connection. The Peanut Statue you see as you come into town has a Jimmy Carter smile. The visitor center was in Jimmy and Rosalyn's high school. He still teaches Sunday school at the Baptist Church when he is in town. Jimmy and Rosalyn built their home in 1960 and it is still their home, with complete secret service.

Billy Carter's gas station is still there, run down and closed, but still there. We walked through the screened, two-story, white farmhouse the Carter kids grew up in, outside of town. Downtown Plains' railroad depot was Jimmy Carter's Presidential Campaign Headquarters in 1976. Denise and I entered a general store and asked if Jimmy ever showed up. The clerk said he occasionally comes in to see how his books are selling.

As President, Jimmy Carter said,

War may sometimes be a necessary evil. But no matter how necessary, it is always evil, never a good. We will not learn how to live together in peace by killing each other's Children.

I wonder if he was thinking of the Civil War Prison Camp, Andersonville and the horrors that happened there when he made that statement. The 26-acre camp, 125 miles south of Atlanta, started taking Union prisoners in February of 1864. It was built as a 10,000-prisoner camp that was more secure than Richmond and had more food sources. The prisoner exchange system broke down between North and South, so the prison population exploded to as many as 33,000 prisoners at a time. Sanitation was nonexistent. The only water was a swampy stream down a sloping hillside and all the camp filth filtered into that water. The stench was unbearable, with the odors held in by double, 15-foot walls built from surrounding pines. The men had only scraps of wood and shreds of cloth to cover holes they dug as shelters. Needless to say, disease ran rampant in the form of dysentery, diarrhea, and scurvy. Thirteen thousand prisoners died there in the camp's 14-month history. Hunger was such a problem that it is said it took seven prisoners to make a shadow. In August of 1864, conditions got so bad that 90 men died in one day.

In the same month, a group of Christian prisoners banded together at the bottom of the hillside and prayed for hours for clean water. They received their answer with a crack and a boom like thunder. They looked down as a spring of water came out of the ground. The camp was still horrendous but the men had clean water, thanks to God's intervention. The spring was called Providence Spring and there is a stone house monument where the spring still runs today. One of the inscriptions on the monument states, "God smote the hillside and gave them drink. Aug. 1864."

The last sad note about this place is that northern citizens were so incensed by what happened at the camp that the commandant Henry Wirz, was brought up on war crimes charges that weren't true. He was just a pawn in the Confederate system. He even tried to get the prisoner exchange system revived to relieve the over-population of the camp. Regardless of his efforts, he was found guilty and became the only Confederate executed after the Civil War.

From the 19th Century, we had to travel back to the 21st Century at our 23-story hotel in the heart of Atlanta's skyscrapers on Wednesday. Thursday morning, November 24th, Thanksgiving Day, Denise and I had to get up well before the sun to catch a ride on MARTA, Atlanta's subway system, a first for us, to get to the Marathon start area under the Olympic rings from the 1996 Summer Olympics. The Atlanta Braves' Turner Field was right across the street.

We 700 marathoners took off at 7:30 AM and headed for the shadows of Atlanta's downtown skyscrapers and Georgia's Capitol building. It was a cool windy day with the sun out and a starting temperature in the lower 40s. After some early hill climbing, the course moved into a rolling section along some parkways. The last six miles made you remember you were doing a marathon with more up hills than down and a stiff headwind. The temperature rose to the mid-50s by the end of the race. I finished in 4 hours and 12 minutes. Good for 298th out of 603 finishers. There were 7,000 in the half marathon. I had completed my 17th state marathon.

Denise and I enjoyed our Thanksgiving Day dinner with all the fixings back at the hotel before heading back to Cable the next day.

Finishing the Atlanta Marathon under the Olympic Rings

Stonehouse monument to Providence Springs and a cut in the landscape in the foreground was the stream for 30,000 prisoners water. The inset shows the monument to suffering in front of Andersonville Cemetery.

Plains, Georgia, Jimmy Carter's hometown

Charlottesville Marathon

Charlottesville, Virginia

I picked the Charlottesville Marathon for my Virginia marathon because I wanted to run through the area three of our Founding Fathers called home. Thomas Jefferson and James Monroe lived in the Charlottesville area and James Madison's home is a little farther north near Orange, Virginia.

These three presidents each made a very important contribution to the establishment of our country. Thomas Jefferson wrote the Declaration of Independence, giving our fight against the British a united purpose. James Madison was the prime mover in developing our Constitution so our federal government had strength without overpowering states. James Monroe is the author of the Monroe Doctrine, ending European efforts to colonize parts of the Americas.

Thomas Jefferson was like a big brother to Monroe and Madison, fifteen years older than James Monroe, and eight years older than James Madison. Jefferson definitely influenced their thinking. He even taught Monroe law. He also talked James Monroe into buying the plantation next to his. The two of them kept a path through the woods open between Monroe's Ash Lawn-Highland front door and Jefferson's Monticello so they could make visual contact.

All three Founding Fathers had their faults. They all spent too much money entertaining and came up short of funds in their retirement years. They all owned slaves, even though they knew slavery was wrong. They also knew we all come up short in doing the right thing.

Madison made this point when he made the statement, "If men were angels, no government would be necessary." Monroe backed up this point when he said, "The best form of government is that which is most likely to prevent the greatest sum of evil."

Thomas Jefferson then came through with this all-encompassing statement: "He who knows best knows how little he knows." Granted Jefferson is talking about general knowledge of the right direction while the other two are talking about doing the right thing, yet they are all talking about the better good of all concerned.

The Charlottesville Marathon organizers didn't know how little they knew about getting the details right in a marathon. Race day, Saturday, April 15, 2006, was hot and humid with a penetrating sun. The organizers couldn't do anything about that. The course was hilly beginning to end, with four miles of gravel road along the way. That was fine with me. The problem was, aid stations ran out of water. I heard they were reusing cups discarded by runners. That shouldn't happen in a race where the temperature hit 88 degrees.

The course left the city for some scenic rural roads, passing some huge homes with horses running through the pastures, and the hazy Blue Ridge Mountains in the background. The problem was, the roads had no shoulder and the traffic was a constant concern. Eating exhaust on a hot, humid day while you are running is not pleasant, let alone safe. When we finally got back to Charlottesville for the last three miles, there was a stretch where we had to run through an outdoor mall area. Tourists and customers were unaware and in some cases became annoyed by the presence of runners. I was totally dead to the world by the time I got to this area and I probably looked like a tourist at times. I was down to walking some of this last stretch through the shoppers. I can't even remember the location of the finish line. I do know that I made it there in 5 hours and 9 minutes. I finished 363rd out of 452 finishers. It wasn't glamorous but I completed my 18th state marathon.

Madison's Montpelier, Monroe's Ash Lawn-Highland, and Jefferson's Monticello

Grandfather Mountain Marathon

Boone, North Carolina

In July of 2006 Denise and I drove southeast to the Blue Ridge Mountains of North Carolina. I was concerned about southern heat and humidity but we found cool, cloudy weather that rarely hit 70 degrees while we were in Daniel Boone's old stomping grounds of Boone, North Carolina. It is definitely a mountainous area, similar to Scotland except for the hardwood and spruce forests that cover the Blue Ridge Mountains and 6,000-foot Grandfather Mountain in particular. The highlands of North Carolina's Avery County have the same mountain views of sprawling valleys, morning mists, waterfalls, and heather of the Scottish Highlands. This is the reason the Scots were drawn to this area, along with a desire to escape religious persecution and a better opportunity to make a living. North Carolina has a larger Scottish population than the country of Scotland. Scottish names like McRae, Buchanan, and Forbes are prevalent in the area.

Once a year the Scottish clans get together at MacRae Meadows on Grandfather Mountain for their Highland Games. During the 2006 marathon 146 clan tents surrounded the East Meadows Track with at least 10,000 people in attendance for the two-day event.

Competitions are held in most track events, including the caber throw, highland wrestling, the kilted mile, hammer throw, and clan tug-of-war. The musical end of the competition includes bag piping, drumming, Highland dancing, and Scottish fiddling. Sheep herding demonstrations and a golf tournament are also a part of the event.

The Grandfather Mountain Marathon on Saturday, July 8, is one of the track and field events. We started at 6:30 AM on the track of Kidd Brewer Stadium at the campus of Appalachian State in Boone. The temperature at the start was 47 degrees. I remember my water bottle falling out when we were still on the track and I had to backtrack through the runners to get it. A little thing like that can sap a person's energy. I got past it and we made our way through town, passing Bojangles Restaurant and the Boone Mall before heading out of town. The route had 1,000 feet of elevation gain and 3,000 feet of climbing with all the ups and downs. The winding road up the mountain had rock formations right into the highway, waterfalls, and 16 ecological communities from the bottom to the top. The race covered a good share of those. The biggest traffic hazard was the drivers unwilling to give us our one foot of shoulder around sharp turns. I remember having a stare-down with one elderly car passenger, probably Scottish, coming toward me but still refusing to give me any space.

When we finally reached the entrance of Grandfather Mountain Park and the Highland Games, we had one more hill to climb as we turned the corner to enter the East Meadow Track. On the way up, a group of Highlanders played "Chariots of Fire" for us. Then we entered the track with at least 10,000 Scottish folks looking on, many from the clan tents and some from the bleachers. In the middle of the track, as we circled, the caber throw event took place. On the other end of the infield was the sheep herding. The peak of Grandfather Mountain oversaw the whole event in the background. It was like entering a fantasyland from the quiet of the run up the mountain, except for the traffic to the festival atmosphere with 10,000 Scots looking on as we finished. The cloudy, cool day never did hit 70. I finished in 4 hours and 36 minutes, which made me the 226th finisher out of 347 who believed they could finish the toughest marathon in the East, and did. I learned later that the marathon was at least a half-mile too long. It was my 19th state marathon.

Finish area of the Grandfather Mountain Marathon in front of the Scottish Clans
Photo by Hugh Morton

Crater Lake Marathon

Crater Lake National Park, Oregon

Five weeks after the Grandfather Mountain Marathon, Denise, Lon, and I flew out to the Pacific Northwest to run the Crater Lake Marathon only one week after the Grand View, Wisconsin weekend. A Saturday 50-mile road bike race is followed by a tough, hilly fifteen-kilometer run on Sunday, in the small northern Wisconsin town. As I look back at this sequence of events now, I realize why Crater Lake was so tough, not to mention that the course requires a runner to add forty minutes to his usual marathon time, if there is such a thing as a normal marathon time.

Crater Lake itself is the deepest lake in the United States and the ninth deepest lake in the world. It fills a five-mile by six-mile crater formed when the huge volcano Mount Mazama exploded about 8,000 years ago. The lake is 1,943 feet deep and maintains its level with 533 inches of snowfall to balance out evaporation. There are no inlets or outlets and it rarely freezes over. It contains Rainbow trout and Kokamee salmon, planted in the late 19th century. Because they are not native, you can catch them without a license.

Wizard Island is a smaller, black, ash covered volcano within the crater. The black surface makes yellow-striped garter snakes easy pickings for predatory birds. Today there are only garter snakes without yellow stripes on the island.

Early Saturday morning, we had to get on a bus at the Rim Village to take us to the start at the Watchman, up on the rim of Crater Lake overlooking the Cascade Range. It was a clear, 40-degree morning when the race started at 7:30 AM. The elevation was about 7,600 feet and the first mile went up from there before we ran six miles downhill. For the first time in my life I felt the effects of elevation sickness. An unsettled stomach went away but reappeared later in the race. Then came an elevation gain of 1,000 feet between miles ten and fourteen. I walked part of this section. Miles fourteen to twenty-two were a welcome downhill. We passed the area where the finish was but we knew the most unforgiving four miles of the course were yet to come. We had to climb 470 feet over two miles on a dirt-logging road before coming back down on the same road to the finish line. There was walking in this section also. The average finish time in this marathon was 4 hours and 41 minutes. I finished in 4 hours and 43 minutes, which was good for 63rd out of 115 finishers. Lon was well ahead of me in a time of 4 hours and 19 minutes. He was the 41st finisher. Crater Lake was my 20th state marathon.

The marathon followed the highway three-quarters the way around Crater Lake.

Lon and I in front of the lodge where the bus took us to the start of the marathon at the Watchman

Gulf Coast Marathon

Gulf Port, Mississippi

Denise and I headed south in November of 2006 with our newly purchased 2003 Hyundai Santa Fe. We were going to be in the area Katrina hit one year earlier. The people of that area thought they could handle any storm after Hurricane Camille in 1969, but they were wrong. Katrina made Camille look like any tropical storm. Waves of 38 feet crashed into the mainland, causing flooding 12 miles inland. People climbed on their roofs to escape the water. Of the 728 homes on the National Registry of Historic Homes on the Bay of St. Louis before Katrina, only 16 remained after the hurricane. The motel where we stayed was still being remodeled from the storm and uprooted trees were still common sights.

The race was held at the NASA Stennis Space Center in Southern Mississippi, just off of I-10, 45 miles east of New Orleans. This is where the booster engines were tested for the Apollo Space Missions. Neil Armstrong and Buzz Aldrin's spaceship's boosters were tested here before they made their trip to land on the moon. The center was named after Mississippi's U.S. Senator John Stennis, who strongly supported the space program and was a U.S. Senator for 41 years.

This area of coastal southeast Mississippi changed from a logging community to a spacecraft-testing center in the 1960s. Now a group of runners was going to cover much of the government facilities' grounds twice in the two-loop Gulf Coast Marathon. The start was in a campground on Lower Gainsville Road. Marathon Saturday was a mostly clear day with temperatures rising quickly from the mid 60s at the 8 AM start. The course was flat with almost no traffic. There were no spectators except at the aid stations. The temperatures quickly made it to the 70s and we welcomed any shade the bordering trees offered. The government provided immaculate concrete roads, which reflected the sun's rays, adding to the tiring heat. I felt like I should have run faster, but it wasn't in me that day. It took me 4 hours and 54 minutes to finish the race. I was 71st out of 128 finishers. The average finish time was 4 hours and 48 minutes. I had my 21st state marathon.

Dwight Eisenhower's boyhood home in Abilene, Kansas

Cold start to the 2007 Abilene Marathon

Eisenhower Marathon

Abilene, Kansas

April 7, 2007 was a record cold day in Abilene, Kansas, with a little drifted snow in the shaded spots. The Eisenhower Marathon started in front of the St. Andrews Parish Hall where a pancake and sausage breakfast had been served before the 7 AM start.

Dwight Eisenhower grew up across the street in a small white house. He loved reading about history, including stories about the Chisholm Trail, which made up the marathon route. Dwight's mother even had to take away his books of our history because chores weren't getting done. Ike did find time to be a sports star in baseball and football in high school. He even stood up for a black player from an opposing team when no one from his team would line up against him because he was black. Dwight knew what it felt like to be treated unfairly, not because he was black but because he was poor, so he was willing to help someone else. He understood what it was like to be, "from the wrong side of the tracks." Ike worked at whatever jobs were available in Abilene. He baked tamales, sold corn, picked apples, and worked on the night shift at the fire department.

West Point saw Ike's potential and offered him a scholarship. He went on to be General of the US Army in WWII and our 34th President.

The Eisenhower Library and Museum are across the street from the marathon start. My immediate concern Saturday morning was the 20-degree temperature with a north wind beginning to build. We had to head south on Hwy. 15, which was the Chisholm Trail one hundred and forty years ago.

It is amazing that a tick, a song with a thousand verses, and Joe McCoy gave the Chisholm Trail and Abilene, Kansas a place in history. Three million head of cattle were sent East from Abilene between 1867 and 1871.

The first longhorns moved north from the pastureland around San Antonio, Texas to the railhead in Sedalia, Missouri, in 1836.

The longhorns carried a tick causing Spanish Fever with close to 100 percent fatality among shorthorn breeds found in Missouri. They passed a law forbidding longhorns in the state. Kansas had a similar law, but they decided to allow longhorns in the western part of the state because there weren't many shorthorn cattle there. Joe McCoy talked the Kansas Pacific Railway into building a spur into Abilene and he built up the town with a bank, hotel, and stockyard office. Then came the cattle, two to three thousand in a cattle drive with ten cowboys keeping them in line. The cowboys had been on the trail two months when they got to Abilene and there was money in their pockets. Abilene got a little wild, with the likes of Wild Bill Hickok trying to keep the peace.

We were running out and back on that same trail in the marathon with a horse rider escort along the way. When I reached the first aid station, I took a drink of water, or I thought I did. I looked in the cup and it was all ice. The Eisenhower Marathon is about the only marathon where you can actually see one aid station to another. The wind picked up along the way, not the temperature. That was fine going out over the rolling hills but coming back, heading into a 20 mph headwind stood me right up, especially across the open fields. I blew through the first half in 2 hours 3 minutes and made it to the finish line in 4 hours and 30 minutes.

It was time for lunch at the Catholic Church. I was 94th out of 155 finishers. This was my 22nd state marathon. A visit to the Eisenhower Library and Museum filled the afternoon before heading home.

Bayshore Marathon

Traverse City, Michigan

Denise and I headed south over the Mackinac Bridge on May 25th of 2007 to Traverse City on Grand Traverse Bay in the southern peninsula of Michigan. After getting my bib and a good meal, I thought I was ready to run in the morning. Monday, Memorial Day turned out to be cool and sunny. We started out at 7 AM from Northwestern Michigan College in the Bayshore Marathon by heading through a residential area before heading north, up the Old Mission Peninsula. A cool breeze blew off Lake Michigan on the right and we saw a mixture of impressive lake homes and wineries on the left. A flat, shaded, and paved road added to the positive effect of the scenery.

The first eight miles went well and I was looking for a good marathon. Bad things started showing up in mile nine. I started feeling pain in my left leg, which usually radiated out from my knee. Then my right leg started to hurt, probably from trying to relieve the pressure in my left leg. Also, a crown in the road, probably added to the leg pain. What started as a positive day turned negative in a hurry. I had to pull off the road every mile and stretch out in the grass so my legs would work again without too much pain. As I was stretching out I watched the runners that I passed and started ahead of pass me by. More negativity. When I got to mile thirteen and the turn around, I started thinking, maybe I can make it. Finally some positive thoughts. During the second half of the race the medical wagon hung over me like a vulture. One time a medic stopped to ask me how I was doing. I was running like Chester of Gunsmoke fame walked and still stopping to stretch every mile. Obviously I wasn't doing so well, but I wasn't going to tell him that. I just kept going and looking for mile markers so I could stop and stretch to hopefully relieve some of the pain. When mile markers 20 and above showed up, I started thinking more positive thoughts, like, I can do this in less than six hours. It isn't going to be great but I'm going to get there. When we got back to the college campus we had to make one trip around their quarter mile track. I found a burst of energy when I got to the track and forgot the pain. The finish line and Denise were in sight. Denise was worried that something was wrong. She was right. After I finished, I stiffened right up and getting back to the car was another challenge. I finished in 5 hours and 25 minutes. Out of the 1,292 finishers there were still 47 finishers behind me. They must have had a long day. I finished my 23rd state marathon and that is what counted for me. The next morning we left the tart cherry capital of the United States and headed home.

Tulsa Route 66 Marathon

Tulsa, Oklahoma

After traveling to Des Moines on Friday night, Denise and I drove to the center of a quiet Tulsa, Oklahoma, on Saturday afternoon. Denise was doing the Route 66 quarter marathon and I was looking for my 24th state marathon.

Sunday, November 18 of 2007 started early for us because we had a little over a mile to walk to reach the 8 AM start of the race. Along the way we past an old church that evangelist Oral Roberts, who had his headquarters in Tulsa, built. A little farther we saw a sign marking Route 66.

Politicians sold the idea of the 2,448 mile paved Route 66 from Chicago, Illinois, to Santa Monica, California, in 1926 by calling it an interregional link connecting rural main streets to urban sprawls. The route passed through the states of Missouri, Kansas, Oklahoma, Texas, New Mexico, and Arizona. To further publicize the highway, the U.S. Highway 66 Association put on a stage foot race in 1928, set up much like the Tour de France bike race. It was called the Bunion Derby and it ran from Ascot Speedway in Los Angeles to Madison Square Garden in New York City. Of the 241 racers from around the world who lined up for the start, 55 finished the race. Andy Hartley Payne, a Cherokee runner from Claremore, Oklahoma, won the race in 573 hours and 4 minutes.

Andy wasn't taken seriously at the start of the race with big name competition, which included race walkers. His hometown Claremore Chamber of Commerce didn't even want to help him, but they finally gave him $75 for the race. The entry fee was $25 and each runner had to have a deposit of $100 for a bus trip home. Andy's dad borrowed the rest of the money Andy needed for the race.

This young runner developed a shuffle, which allowed him to keep a good pace without causing leg pain. Andy's plan was to stay near the world famous leaders and let them burn out before he took the lead. After several runners fell out of the race in the early going, Andy found himself in the lead over the Arizona high country, but tonsillitis and a fever slowed him down. He regained the lead by the time the race made it to Oklahoma. Businesses and schools closed in Andy's honor during the race while several Oklahomans wanted his autograph or to run with him. Because of all the attention, he lost the lead again by the time they reached Tulsa. He reclaimed the lead when he came to his hometown of Claremore, with Will Rogers among those out to greet Andy. Collisions with motorcycles and cars, health issues, and injuries brought the race field down to 80 runners by this point. After wearing out five pairs of rubber-soled shoes and living in a tent, Andy won the race by fifteen hours and collected $25,000. He used the money to pay off the mortgage on the family farm, built a new house, and invested the rest in land that went down in value. That worked out for Andy, though, because gas and oil were found on the land.

Before the day of the interstate highway, Route 66 was the way to see America. Now a few of us are seeing America by doing a marathon in each state.

Denise and I made it to the start area of the Tulsa Route 66 Marathon to hear the race director's opening prayer and Pledge of Allegiance. I took off my hat and forgot that I put my energy gels for the race under my hat. I was looking around for them after the prayer, not knowing I was balancing them on my head. Denise and another racer got quite a laugh out of my accidental comedy act.

The race was an out and back with temperatures starting at about 50 degrees and rising to 68 on a cloudy day. We ran along the Arkansas River for sometime, crossed it, and returned on the same route before passing through a residential area. The last three miles were very hilly as we went through a wooded park. Those hills just kept growing as we worked our way up, especially when my body was totally gone at miles 23 to 26.

Denise had a good quarter marathon, running all the way. She finished the race in 1 hour and 23 minutes. She was 348th out of 484 finishers. I finished the marathon in 4 hours and 27 minutes. I was the 558th finisher out of 1058.

Lincoln National Guard Marathon

Lincoln, Nebraska

Denise's sister and brother-in-law are probably sick of us using their home in Des Moines as a stopping place on our way to a marathon. This time we were headed to Lincoln, Nebraska. We got to Lincoln Saturday, May 3 of 2008. At the University Natural History Museum, I picked up my race bib. Dan Karnazes, the ultramarathoner, was the special speaker. I remember him saying he ran on the highway's white lines when he competed in the 135 mile Badwater Ultramarathon as it crossed Death Valley in 130-degree heat, because he found that the black pavement was actually hot enough to melt the bottom of his running shoes.

That evening we enjoyed a spaghetti dinner at the University of Nebraska's Quarterback Club. I took a side trip into the Cornhusker Stadium and looked at the Nebraska Heisman Trophy Museum. The museum included Johnny Rodger's trophy. He was voted the team's player of the century, and his jersey number 20 was retired.

The University of Nebraska has had a diverse range of graduates since its 1869 beginning. General "Black Jack" Pershing, the only person to be promoted to General of the Armies in his own lifetime, graduated from Nebraska, as did Johnny Carson from the Tonight Show. The billionaire Warren Buffet also calls Nebraska his alma mater.

Sunday morning, May fourth, was sunny and cool. The marathon started at 7 AM on the brick streets of the University. The race proceeded through nearby neighborhoods before heading downtown and past the capital. Miles six through eight were crowded because we were on the narrow Hwy. 2-bike path with the half marathoners. The aid stations were somewhat unique, with National Guard help and cups with lids and straws. The course was mainly flat with a few grinding inclines. We ran the last five miles of the first half back to the University where we lost the half marathoners. I finished the first half in 2 hours and 3 minutes.

Denise met me at the halfway point with another pair of shoes. The change helped relieve the foot tendon pain I was experiencing. I later learned the cause, plantar fasciitis. The second half of the race was an out and back to Holmes Lake, with a lonely feel to it without the half marathoners around. The temperature remained cool, probably in the mid 60s. I got back to the University and the finish line in 4 hours and 27 minutes. I had my 25th state marathon and was the 558th finisher out of 1170 total.

Hatfield and McCoy Marathon

Williamson, West Virginia

Denise and I drove through coal country in Kentucky to the hills of Williamson, West Virginia, in June of 2008. It was sunny, hot, and humid with 90-plus temperatures. I picked up my race packet and we went to the Hatfield-McCoy spaghetti dinner at the Sycamore Inn in Williamson. After dinner, Dave Hatfield, yes he is one of the Hatfields as well as race director, told us what to expect on the racecourse the next morning. Dave was just the introduction to Devil Hatfield and Randall McCoy, reenacting the feud, squirrel rifles in hand. These two actors brought the 1863-1891feud to life. It started with a few McCoys joining the Union Army while the Hatfields were mostly strong Confederate supporters during the Civil War. Then there was the Hatfield hog that was claimed by the McCoys. Finally, Johnson Hatfield jilted Roseanne McCoy. On top of that, friction grew between the two families because the Hatfields were fairly well-off lumbermen in West Virginia while the McCoys were poor dirt farmers in Kentucky.

Saturday, June 14[th,] was cloudy, humid, and 70 degrees. The marathon was taking shape at the Food City parking lot in Goody, Kentucky. We all watched the sky and prayed for rain to break the heavy air and heat. The 7 AM shotgun start took us out of Goody and toward coal country near Hardy, Kentucky on a steady incline. The older well-worn homes were built right out to the edge of the road. Either that, or the road was built right up to the homes. The incline continued to the foot of Blackberry Mountain and feud country. This is where Talbert, Bud, and Pharmer McCoy were tied up to trees and shot by the Hatfields for the Election Day stabbing of Ellison Hatfield, brother of Devil Anse Hatfield. The graves are still there. At the foot of Blackberry Mountain is also the location of Rev. Anderson Hatfield's home. He was the judge in the disputed hog trial held in his home in 1878.

Time to forget history, make the one mile climb of Blackberry Mountain, and glide down the fast steep descent before passing through the rolling Appalachian Hills of the last five miles of the first half of the marathon. The halfway point was Matewan, West Virginia where the largest gunfight in US history took place in 1920.

71

The second half of the course took us through more Appalachian hill country, crossing the Tug River, and an hour-long thunderstorm to cool us down. The cool rain was a welcome trade off for soggy shoes. The hills, heat, and humidity took their toll on me by mile eighteen and then I had to cross the swinging bridge in the Tug Valley Golf Course. I felt woozy and that bridge kept moving, not easy to cross. I managed to pull myself together for the last wet miles into Williamson. Randall McCoy and Devil Hatfield were there to greet us. It seemed fitting to have my picture taken with those guys so I did.

I finished in 4 hours and 32 minutes. The average finish time was 4 hours and 49 minutes. I was 89th out of 210 finishers. I had finished my 26th state marathon.

Denise and I ate a pork sandwich lunch at the finish, which was included in the marathon deal. After lunch we went back to Matewan to see what secrets that community held. We sat down on a Main Street bench and looked over the town. A big, older miner sat next to us and started telling me how well his son was doing driving heavy equipment in the mines, making $20 an hour. He was obviously very proud. Then he asked me if we had seen the bullet holes in the back of the nearby building from the 1920 shootout. We went back to take a look and I tried to place things as they must have been on that May, 1920 day. I know the train pulled in to Matewan with Baldwin-Felts agents on board, hired by mine owners to evict fired miners from company housing. The agents didn't know miners were hiding in buildings and on rooftops, waiting for them, along with Sheriff Sid Hatfield. The first shot is still a mystery, but when it was all over there were seven dead agents, two dead miners, and a dying mayor Caleb Testerman. Some claimed Sheriff Hatfield shot the mayor in the shootout because he wanted his wife. That was never proven, but the sheriff did later marry the mayor's wife. Sid Hatfield and the miners were found innocent of murder so Albert Felts had his agents shoot and kill the Sheriff and his deputy on the courthouse steps one year later.

On a happier note, we watched a tug-of-war across the Tug River with the Hatfields on one side and the McCoys on the other. As I remember, the Hatfields got wet this time but that is a lot easier to take than a bullet from a shootout.

Election Day fight location along the Hatfield-McCoy
Marathon route

Matewan, location of the halfway point of the Hatfield and
McCoy Marathon and the largest shootout in US history

Randall McCoy, Devil Hatfield, and I at the finish line in
Williamson, West Virginia

Hatfield-McCoy tug-of-war on the Tug River

Jay Mountain Marathon

Jay, Vermont

The Ultramarathon Left Unfinished

Lon, Denise, and I drove to Vermont the end of July, 2008. The bad tendon in my foot was really making itself known. Running became a limp and two miles was a major effort, not to mention a 33-mile ultramarathon. We already had paid for some of the trip, so I was going to try to finish this race.

We drove to the small community of Jay, Vermont, in the woods of the Green Mountains. Only five miles from Canada, 3,681-foot Jay Peak shadowed the area in the background.

The morning of the race I still hurt, so I told a sports medicine tech from Montreal what I was dealing with. He said he could fix me up. He worked over my foot pretty good, but 100 yards into the race the pain returned. We were running through ankle to knee-deep mud. It actually felt soothing on the foot and the word "running" was an overstatement in this case. One hillside was so slimy and steep, they had placed ropes to help us to the top. Next came a mountain stream swollen with seven days of rain. There were good-sized rocks in the stream that we had to maneuver around while we made our way against the current. To make things interesting, we had to go through a three or four-foot-diameter culvert, directing the stream under a road. Once out of the stream, there was more mud through the woods.

Finally I reached the foot of Jay Peak and the shoe exchange aid station. Dry shoes and socks felt good after wearing shoes that had gone through eleven miles of mud and water. We had a two-mile climb up the mountain without any switchbacks, just up and steep. At the top a food station and a view of the Green Mountains awaited us. The trip down the mountain on the other side was partly on slippery slate, and steep. I slipped and fell back, but bounced right back up with the steep slope. At the bottom, more mud and another mile of mountain stream just waiting. So much for dry shoes.

When we got out of the stream, there were actually some fields to cross. Solid ground felt great and I tried to limp and run the best I could. A skydiving instructor from Colorado joined me at this point and Denise met us at the mile-eighteen aid station. She told us the officials were going to give us an extra half hour to make the cut-off because of the excess mud and water. I was feeling kind of confident about pulling this thing off, but then came another stream, actually a river about 40 feet wide with huge boulders, fast current, and a two-part waterfall totaling about 10 feet. The current going with us was not helpful because it had a tendency to take our balance. Falling was a constant concern. I lost the skydiver along this stretch, or he lost me. A girl went over the waterfall and almost drowned if a couple of other racers hadn't helped. After about a mile of the river, it was time to get on dry land again but not for long, as we had to cross a three-quarter mile beaver pond. Orange flags marked the dirty water at each turn. I would be walking along on swamp grass, one foot under water, and the next step would be four feet down and chest deep water without warning. Every step was a surprise. Finally, dry ground appeared at the end of the pond and a wooded area. Not long after, there was another river about 200 feet wide with a rope strung across. Firemen remained on each side to make sure no one drowned. I asked the dumb question, "Can I wade across?" The firemen said the first step would be all right but the next step would be about a 20-foot drop. I grabbed the rope and made my way across, hanging on for dear life, being the wonderful swimmer that I am. I sat and looked at the river on the far side while catching my breath before climbing the hill into another wooded area.

About two miles later I saw the high bush blueberries that marked the 25-mile aid station and the cut-off point. The race director was there to inform us of our status in the race. He came up to me and said, "You know, your time isn't good enough." I was too tired to say anything or care. Several others with the same problem were directed to an old wooden trailer with side panels. The old trailer kind of added to the rotten feeling that was building from not making the cut-off. About twenty of us got in the trailer. I heard there were about 100 total that didn't make the cut-off. I'm sure water and mud conditions added to that number. Talking to some of the others in the trailer on the way back to Jay, they thought I should have just run another one and two tenths mile to get my Vermont marathon. I knew deep down that wouldn't settle with me. It certainly wouldn't fly with the 50 States Club. I would be back to Vermont in the future.

When we got back to Jay, Denise was there with a worried smile. Lon made the cut-off; he was ahead of me all day. He came in to the finish line in Jay about one hour later. It must have been a proud feeling to finish such an event. It is something I'll never know, because the next year they cancelled the event. Lon said the last eight miles weren't that bad, with the only obstacle being a loose sandy area.

This is the only race I entered that I couldn't finish. It still was an incredible experience. It was billed as the toughest event in America. You wouldn't get any argument from Lon or me.

Lon at the finish of the Jay Mt. Ultra. Notice the time.

Quad Cities Marathon

Moline, Illinois

The Quad Cities marathon's attraction to me was about the geography. I would have a chance to run through four cities, in two states, and cross the Mississippi River twice. These towns got their start as trading locations for the Sauk and Fox Indians. Later they were a stopping point for steamboats before they had to deal with river rapids farther north. In the twentieth century they were an agricultural equipment center. As the towns grew, they grew together. International Harvester, Case IH, and John Deere all had plants here in the center of farm country.

The race was centered at the John Deere Commons in Moline, Illinois. After picking up our race bags, we carbo-loaded on spaghetti. After supper Denise and I listened and watched 85-year-old Helen Klein tell us about her running career. She literally hopped on top of the picnic table to get everyone's attention. She is a great-grandmother and a retired nurse. She started running in her backyard and took last in her first ten-mile race. Since then Helen has completed 100 marathons, 140 ultramarathons, and set 75 American and World records in distance running in her age class. And here she was, doing the half marathon at the Quad Cities.

Sunday morning, September 28 of 2008 was a cloudy, cool (60s), but humid race day. The race started at 7:30 AM. Half marathoners, and shorter distance races all started with the marathon making a crowded first crossing of the Mississippi River from Moline to Bettendorf, Iowa, one mile into the race. The marathon route took us from Bettendorf, along the Mississippi, to Davenport, Iowa, the largest of the Quad Cities. From here we crossed the Mississippi again to Rock Island, Illinois. There weren't many hills on the route except for going over bridges. We crossed over to Arsenal Island for miles 13 to 20. It was quiet out there on this typical Sunday, but weekdays saw lots of traffic since it is the largest government owned producer of weapons and the largest employer in the Quad Cities. We crossed back to Moline, Illinois, for a six-mile out and back along the Mississippi to finish the marathon at the John Deere Common. I finished in 4 hours and 49 minutes. I was the 520th finisher out of a total 689. Now I know I wasn't a top finisher but they didn't have a finisher medal for us because they ran out. That should not happen to anyone who completes a marathon. I talked to the son of the race director and let him know I was very disappointed. Not long after the announcer made it plain that those who didn't receive a medal would get one in the mail and I did. Illinois was my 27th state marathon.

Las Vegas Marathon

Las Vegas, Nevada

In Ben Franklin's later years he made the statement, "The Constitution only gives people the right to pursue happiness. You have to catch it yourself." Happiness obviously means different things to different people. The accomplishment of completing a marathon is a part of happiness for me. The friendship Denise and I gained when we met Jim and Diana Heinz at the Whiskey Row Marathon in Prescott, Arizona, earlier is also a big part.

Jim and Diana invited us to their home in Las Vegas, Nevada, so I could do the Las Vegas Marathon in December of 2008. They met us at McCarron Airport and drove us around the racecourse after we picked up my race packet. Jim would have done the race with me but his leg was hurting and he had already done the marathon several times. After touring the course, we went back to Jim and Diana's for a spaghetti dinner and a good night's rest.

Jim took me downtown to the start area in front of the Mandalay Hotel early the next morning. Robin Leach, from the television show "The Rich and Famous" was the announcer. The race got under way in the dark with a fireworks display at a little after 6 AM on Sunday, December 7 of 2008. We ran down the Las Vegas Strip for five and one-half miles with plenty of lights so we could see our way in the 40-degree morning air. There were about 200 Elvises dressed up and running the race. Elvis always said he loved Las Vegas and it was quite clear that Las Vegas wouldn't forget him. Several young ladies in the marathon wore wedding veils. There was a special aid station where couples could stop and get married or renew their vows and continue the race. Forty couples did just that.

From the Strip we headed to the suburbs of Las Vegas. Some young people along the way reminded us that "Jesus Saves."

The course was flat, the sky remained gray, and the temperatures stayed in the fifties. There was only water and Gatorade at the aid stations, and I needed something else. My stomach was talking to me and it wasn't good. At mile 18 Denise, Diana, and Jim were out along the course. I was hoping they would have a banana or something, but no luck. The last eight miles back to the downtown area were tough. A few antacids are all I had to calm my stomach. I made it back to the Mandalay Hotel and the finish line in 4 hours and 22 minutes. I was the 1613th finisher out of a total 3517. Lack of food finally took its toll and I ended up in the marathon sick room for a few minutes before they would release me. They offered me an I.V., but I didn't think that would be necessary.

Later that day Jim and Diana took us to the Venetian, a 4,000-room hotel with a river running among the shops and restaurants of the building. You can take an indoor or outdoor gondola ride, gondolier and all. After dinner we went by the Bellagio Hotel to watch the dancing fountains out front in the quarter-mile-long lake. They are choreographed to lighting and music in a water symphony.

It all made for a memorable 28th marathon weekend.

The Glass City Marathon

Toledo, Ohio

Denise and I mixed a family visit with a marathon weekend at the end of April, 2009. We flew into Detroit. Miriam and Dick, Denise's sister and brother-in-law, made the hour drive from Toledo to take us to their home for a pasta dinner. After dinner I tried running a couple of miles on a bike trail to see how my knees were doing.

After a good night's rest, Dick took me to the start area early the next morning. The location was a little uncertain because there was little evidence of a marathon in front of the downtown hotel where it was supposed to start. This seemed strange for a marathon that had been around for 33 years. Runners began to congregate, looking for the exact location. Finally we were told a line across the street marked the start line and we were ready for the 7 AM start of the Glass City Marathon.

Toledo is known as the Glass City because a lot of the glass industry is centered there. Windows, windshields, fiberglass insulation, and glass art are produced there. Libby Glass, Owens Corning, and John Mansville all have companies in Toledo. Edward Libby even started a glass museum there in 1901, with 30,000 glass objects in it. Today the museum is world famous.

As the race began, we ran through the streets of Toledo. I remember passing the Toledo Mud Hen's baseball stadium, neatly tucked between some large buildings. It was a very up-to-date looking ballpark. The breeze that started with us became a strong head wind and the temperature quickly rose from the low 70s through the first half of the race. We ran along the Maumee River where several fishermen were crowding the banks, trying to get in on the end of, probably the largest river bound walleye run east of the Mississippi River.

The second half of the race had a strong tail wind for a good share of the way. The problem for me was that the temperature continued to rise to 86 degrees and fighting the headwind in the first half of the race had taken a toll. The volunteers at the aid stations did a great job for us but they couldn't bring back my energy level. Walking with running was the best I could do in the second half. I wanted to kind of float along with the wind pushing me, but I just couldn't make much happen and I ended up walking more than I wanted to. When the finish line was finally in sight, Dick joined me for a bit of the push to the line. I finished in 5 hours and 13 minutes. I was 252nd out of 293 finishers. This was my 29th state marathon and several weeks later all finishers received a glass mug in the mail to commemorate the Glass City Marathon.

Discovery Marathon

Port Angeles, Washington

The Discovery Marathon is on the Olympic Peninsula, a magical place in my mind. The race started in Sequim, Washington, which has a Mediterranean climate and receives about 20 inches of rain a year. It rarely snows and rarely hits 80 degrees. Seventy-five miles away, on the west side of the Olympic Mountains, the Hoh Rainforest is found. It receives 170 inches of rain a year. Mt. Olympus, at 7,962 feet, is the tallest mountain in the range. Its elevation is deceptive. It's really just as tall as Pikes Peak, but Pikes Peak sits on a 6000-foot plateau and Mt. Olympus sits at sea level on the Pacific Ocean. Mt. Olympus has a lot of power, making the Pacific drop most of its moisture on the west coast of Washington and the Olympic Mountains, where there are 266 glaciers. This leaves the coast of the Strait of Juan de Fuca in the rain shadow. The Strait itself is known for its temperamental weather that can build waves over thirty feet. A 29-year-old named Bert Thomas swam across the eighteen-mile strait in 1955 in just over eleven hours. He started in Port Angeles, where the marathon would end, and finished in Victoria, British Columbia.

The marathon crossed Klallam tribal lands. The Klallam people have built some colorful and interesting totem poles telling of their culture and beliefs. I visited the shop where a carver hired by the Klallam was working on a pole in Jamestown, Washington. Totems quite often feature the Thunderbird at the top, because it is said to control all of nature's activities. When he flaps his wings, we hear thunder.

Sunday morning, June 7 of 2009 was cool (upper 40s) and cloudy for the 9AM marathon start from Carrie Park in Sequim. Denise was running the 5km over in Port Angeles. We ran out of Sequim to the high point, two miles into the race. From there the route took us about seven miles around the Sequim area where we enjoyed fields of lavender, which does well in this climate. Back in Sequim, we followed the streets past a shopping center where traffic was being held up for us to pass. An elderly lady patiently waited her chance to turn into the shopping entrance until I came in the line of runners. She just decided it was her chance to turn in; I don't know how she missed me. The lady runner behind me screamed, thinking I was hit.

After that excitement, I appreciated the Olympic Discovery Trail through the woods.

At about mile 16 a series of hills showed up. They had size and could be steep. I started running with a young guy, probably about 20. I don't remember if he caught up to me or I caught up to him, but we went back and forth through this section of hills before he lost me. Finally we made it to the outskirts of Port Angeles and the last five miles right on the shore of the Strait of Juan de Fuca. It was on this stretch that a playful otter popped up to check out all the runners. I understand whales, seals, and Klallam tribal canoes are all possible to see out in the strait.

Finally I could see the finish line. I finished in 4 hours and 26 minutes, which placed me as the 198th out of 352 finishers. The average finish time was 4 hours and 34 minutes. Denise completed the 5km, which included a grinding uphill in the middle.

Then I noticed that young guy I had run with for a while with his family. Lo and behold, his mother was Evelyn Wonderly (Ludzack), who grew up just down the hill from me in our hometown of Cable, WI, population 227. Amazing, making unexpected connections 2,000 miles from home and completing my 30th state marathon.

Coming into the Port Angeles finish of the Discovery Marathon along the Strait of Juan de Fuca

The young guy I crossed paths with in the
marathon on one side and his mother, who I
grew up with back in Cable on the other.

The Olympic Mountains bring all the variation
in climate to the Olympic Peninsula.

The route of the Freedom Run Marathon into Harpers Ferry with the Engine House that served as John Brown's fort in his short-lived revolution in the inset

Freedom Run

Shepherdstown, West Virginia

I have a problem with patience. When Lon and I got to the Minneapolis Airport at 5 AM, Friday, Oct. 2 of 2009 and found our flight canceled, I had a problem waiting three hours for the next flight. We finally reached Washington, DC, during rush hour. I tried to tell Lon we needed to watch signs closely or we would get off course. We ended up in the Embassy District with SUVs pulling out in front of us at will. That put us in position to follow the setting sun to Shepherdstown, West Virginia. We were just in time to get in on the end of the pasta dinner and pick up our race bibs for the Freedom Run Marathon. We stayed in Hagerstown, Maryland, which meant getting on the road at 5 AM the next morning to get back to Shepherdstown and catch the marathon bus over to the 7 AM start at the Harpers Ferry Visitor Center. It was a hilly, curvy, narrow back road. If you weren't familiar with the road you would either be in the ditch or lost.

The sun put in its appearance at about the same time as the start of the Freedom Run Marathon, one-quarter mile from the visitor center. The race would unquestionably be a run through Civil War History. We started with a two-mile out and back to Murphy's Farm where Confederate General A.P. Hill forced the surrender of 12,000 Union troops September 15, 1862, after Stonewall Jackson's siege of Harpers Ferry. Stonewall Jackson had cut loose with about 50 cannons from the hills surrounding the town to convince the Union force the struggle was useless. Once we got back to the highway the marathon took a steady descent down to the town of Harpers Ferry.

Harpers Ferry is located on the junction of the Shenandoah and Potomac Rivers. George Washington chose it as a small arms arsenal back in 1796. John Brown led his small force, including two of his sons, to capture the small arms in that arsenal to arm his "hoped for" army of escaped slaves in October of 1859. We ran by the Engine House where John Brown held out against the Robert E. Lee-led army, before he was forced to surrender.

We ran out of Harpers Ferry on an iron bridge, crossing the Potomac River on to a shaded trail, running along the river for about nine miles. At about mile 11 I noticed Lon up ahead. He had left me behind at Murphy's Farm. He stopped at an outhouse at mile 13 and I left him behind. I climbed out of the shaded river trail up the first of many long, steep Maryland hills on Miller Sawmill Rd into sunny Antietam Battlefield.

We ran through about six miles of the battlefield in reverse order of the way the battle unfolded on that September day in 1862. First, we passed the bridge, still in place over Antietam Creek, where the Confederate troops had the advantage on a hillside, raining down deadly fire on General Burnside's forces as they tried to cross the bridge. Later, we ran by the still visible sunken road. It brought to mind midday of the battle in 1862. The Southern forces had their positions in the sunken road and were able to mow down the advancing Northern units so that it appeared they were disappearing into the ground. Finally, the Union forces got smart and moved around the open end of the sunken road and annihilated the southerners. Farther north, we ran by the area where the battle began the morning of September 17, 1862. It was in a cornfield where Confederate and Union soldiers probed about, looking for the enemy and shooting at any movement. In the end, not one cornstalk was left standing. Bullets had leveled every stalk and hundreds of men lay dead or wounded.

At the end of the day, the battle was a draw with both sides staring at each other on two of those hills we were fighting our way up and down in the marathon. Three thousand six hundred-fifty soldiers lost their lives there. I told another runner that the soldiers suffering usually didn't last long, but ours lasted hours out in the warm autumn sun. At about this point, Lon passed me again.

From Antietam we followed the shoulder of a busy highway back to Shepherdstown, sucking in car fumes. The finish line was at the Shepherd University football stadium. I finished in 4 hours and 42 minutes, three minutes behind Lon. My guts were killing me at the finish, but I recovered for a smorgasbord dinner at Golden Corral. I was 161st out of 256 finishers. This would be my 31st state marathon. At least that is what I thought at the time. I'll explain later.

Space Coast Marathon

Cocoa Village, Florida

Abraham Lincoln made the statement, "Most folks are as happy as they make up their minds to be." Denise and I had a shuttle bus driver demonstrate that thought to the fullest as we headed to the Minneapolis airport, about 4:30 in the morning. We were headed to Orlando, Florida, for a marathon and Thanksgiving. Our driver had previously had an aneurysm and almost died. He felt so grateful to be alive, even though his memory wasn't perfect, he had to tell his story to everyone he took to the airport. He made clear how fortunate we all are for every day we have to live. His effervescent disposition gave us a positive outlook during the whole trip.

Rachel, Denise's niece, picked us up at the airport in Orlando and took us to her and her husband Dirk's home in Palm Bay, Florida. She has quite the resume, working on secret projects for the air force. Denise and Rachel were going to do the Space Coast half marathon together while I did the marathon.

Denise's twin brother, who is Rachel's dad, and the rest of his family, were also flying down for Thanksgiving. Rachel and Dirk put together a great meal and we all sat around a campfire in their backyard after, telling family secrets while watching the stars.

Friday and Saturday we became Florida tourists with Rachel as our tour guide. We visited St. Augustine; our nation's oldest continuously lived-in European settlement. It is 42 years older than Jamestown. It had to fight for its existence, like most settlements. The native Indians didn't want to be Spanish subjects and the English sent raiders, such as Sir Francis Drake, who decimated the place. Saturday we all picked up our race packets and Denise was able to pick up last minute race necessities at the expo. Later we went down by the beach, which was a little cool, being November.

Sunday morning started early. We had to be at the start in Cocoa Village for the 6 AM start. Marathoners and half marathoners took off to the north together in the dark. The first couple of miles were crowded before it thinned out and the sky lightened up. The temperature was probably in the 50s under a sunny sky with low humidity, making good running weather. We ran along Indian River,

91

which is really part of the ocean. Some runners saw dolphins jumping. The land beyond Indian River is called Merritt Island, home to Cape Canaveral and the NASA Space Program. It was in the process of closing down, driving unemployment up and house values down. Not a good situation for those living here. On the landside of the course was a series of oceanside homes that told us someone has money around here. The route was a winding out and back, bringing the half marathoners to their finish near the start area. The rest of us marathoners continued to the south for another out and back. Denise and Rachel finished in 3 hours and 11 minutes. The second half of the race was much quieter without the half marathoners.

The aid stations were great, equipped with all the gels and drinks we needed. They had a real competition for the best costumes with a space theme. One aid station had a Star Trek theme, the next Star Wars. I finally made it back to the start area for the second time, which was my finish in 4 hours and 25 minutes. The temperature had risen to about 70 but that didn't feel bad. I was 367th out of 659 finishers. I had my 32nd state marathon on November 29, 2009.

We went back to Rachel's to clean up before heading to the airport and flying home. There was school the next day.

Denise and I proudly display hard earned medals in a state that has everything from 16th Century St. Augustine to the 20th Century space program.

My Space Coast Marathon finish at Cocoa Village

Fargo Marathon

Fargo, North Dakota

I have to borrow words from Theodore Roosevelt again. He said, "Believe you can and you're halfway there." No matter what marathon a person does, it is a stretch for the human body, so a positive attitude is crucial for success. Teddy Roosevelt also said, " Do what you can, with what you have, where you are."

Fargo, North Dakota, puts those words into practice. It is a community of 113,000 that started as a steamboat stop in 1870 on the north running Red River. Citizens of Fargo have to deal with the Red River's spring flooding as it passes right through the city center. They know how to work together as a community to limit the flood damage, moving a million sandbags to protect their town. The people of Fargo also know how to work as a community to put on a very successful marathon, even though they are far from any other population center. There were 21,500 participants in all events at the 2010 marathon. Many more Fargoans were enthusiastic volunteers.

On May 21 of 2010, I drove across Minnesota to Fargo for their marathon. Jim Heinz, passing through Cable from another marathon, rode along for support. We attended the pasta dinner, where the special speaker was a runner who had survived an aneurysm and yet was running the marathon.

Saturday morning, May 22 was a rainy cool day. I started the race wearing a windbreaker but that lasted only a mile before it got so warm I took it off and tied it around my waist for the rest of the race. Some of the race went through tree-shaded residential streets with several turns. The course is billed as flat and fast, with several bands playing to the musical tastes of most, from rock to bagpipes. I must admit a leaning toward the bagpipes. About ten miles into the race, the sun broke through the clouds, warming us. We headed across the Red River and the Minnesota-North Dakota border into Moorhead, Minnesota and Concordia College. This was a quiet peaceful stretch of the race. By mile twenty the clouds took over again and the temperature dropped. Jim came out to run the last three miles with me. Finally we could see the Fargodome ahead, which meant the finish line. The Fargodome is an indoor stadium that hosts many events, including the North Dakota State Bison football games. The course goes down and into the stadium where you can see yourself finish on the Jumbotron. I finished in 4 hours and 37 minutes. That was 1304th out of 1885 finishers in the marathon. Fargo was my 33rd state marathon.

Finishing at the Lake Placid Marathon

Jim Heinz at the Lake Placid finish line

Lake Placid Marathon

Lake Placid, New York

In mid-June of 2010, Lon, Denise and I stopped at the home of James Garfield, our twentieth President, and his wife Lucretia, in Mentor, Ohio on our way to the Lake Placid Marathon. Lucretia seemed to have taken to heart her husband James's words when he said, "A pound of pluck is worth a ton of luck." He also said, "Man can't live by bread alone, he needs peanut butter."

Lucretia showed pluck when she daily took care of James as he lingered two months after being shot by a deranged government job seeker four months after he took office in 1881. The newspapers made mention of her efforts and Americans took notice. She ended up with $360,000 from charitable citizens when James died in September of that year. She also received $5,000 a year from her husband's Congressional pension. She lived well.

Now I'm not sure what James meant by peanut butter, but I'm going with the idea that Lucretia used some of the money to add on to her home for the first Presidential Library for James Garfield. This room definitely speaks of his life and the second shortest term as President.

That evening we drove into New York and watched the color show, presented by the lighting on our most powerful waterfalls, the 165-foot Niagara Falls, a good way to celebrate my retirement from teaching.

Jim and Diana Heinz met us in Lake Placid the next day. We watched Olympic hopefuls ski down Whiteface Mountain on water-coated plastic shingles before making their double somersault into a huge pool at the bottom of the mountain.

Behind the skating oval, which is the finish of the marathon, is the Olympic Center that houses the rink where the 1980 U.S. Hockey Team won the gold medal, known as the Miracle on Ice. Local skaters were using the rink when we visited.

Sunday morning, June 13 of 2010, was race day for the Lake Placid Marathon. It was a cool overcast morning when we took off from the start, circling the lake. Near the end of this loop there were two steep hills about a quarter-mile-long each. Those hills put a weak feeling in your legs if you try to tackle them too vigorously. There were water stops every mile or so. I remember one African American volunteer who seemed truly impressed with what we marathoners were accomplishing by running 26 miles. It made me feel pretty special. We went out of town for the second time through the woods with a feeling we were really in the Adirondack backcountry. We came back into town for the last time facing an uphill that must have wound through a residential area for about a half-mile with some serious grade. Finally at the top, we were at the speed skating oval in front of the Olympic Center and the finish line. I finished in 4 hours and 29 minutes; Lon had an excellent marathon with a time of 4 hours and 11 minutes. Jim Heinz was a concern, because they said there was a six-hour limit on finishing. I rested 45 minutes and went back out on the course to find him. He was about a mile out with fifteen minutes to go and that huge uphill. I tried to be an encouragement, as the time got shorter. He made it with about two minutes to spare. It was a memorable 34th state marathon.

Three tired runners

New Hampshire Marathon

Bristol, New Hampshire

Boston lived up to the down side of driving after Denise and I landed at Logan Airport the last day of September, 2010. We had to deal with traffic jams and parking in a parking ramp where the attendant takes your keys and parks your car in a space that is more like a piece in a puzzle than a line of cars. I wondered if I'd ever see that rental car again. When we returned to find our car after visiting the North Church and Old Ironsides, we were confronted with a $40 parking fee, not to mention the attendant had to work his magic just to get our car out of that mass of vehicles. He did and we were on our way with a lighter pocket book.

The next day on our way north to New Hampshire, we stopped at a Shaker Village and enjoyed pot roast and squash biscuits for lunch. Later that day we entered Bristol, New Hampshire, the home of the New Hampshire Marathon. We picked up our race packets and had a spaghetti dinner in the community of about 3,000. Denise was doing their 10 km.

Bristol is a tourist town because of Newfound Lake, the fourth largest lake in New Hampshire. It is two-and-a-half miles wide by six miles long. Tourism has been important since the mid-eighteen hundreds, when steamboats plied the lake.

Race day, October 2nd was cool (50s) and partly cloudy. My 35th state marathon started in front of the Bristol school and ran out of town to a two-to-three-mile uphill stretch as we started our trek around Newfound Lake. We continued along the pine-lined rolling road into a head wind that kept it cool, but we always felt the friction of the moving air. At mile fourteen and the race turn-around, there was another one of those half mile uphills to get our attention before we headed back toward Bristol with a tail wind and rolling hills on the south side of the lake. The last two miles were downhill as we ran back into Bristol and the finish behind the school.

Denise climbed that three-mile uphill as she left town on the 10 km. and returned to town with a downhill tail wind. She finished in 1 hour 18 minutes.

I finished in 4 hours and 23 minutes, which placed me 102nd out of 240 finishers in the marathon. The average finish time was 4 hours and 36 minutes.

Top, the Boston skyline from the deck of Old Ironsides.
Rounding the last corner in Bristol, NH, and, bottom, the finish line of the New Hampshire Marathon

Mid South Marathon

Wynne, Arkansas

The Mid South Marathon is held in Wynne, Arkansas, a town of about eight thousand that got its start from a derailed train. In 1882 a train left the tracks in northeast Arkansas. One of the boxcars that had been on its side, and the wheels taken, was set upright and made into a rail station. A rail-centered town grew up around the station and was named Wynne after Jessie Watkins Wynne. He was a 21-year-old who had been made captain in the Confederate Army after he led his Union captors into Confederate lines and made the captors his prisoners.

November 6 of 2010, was race day in that same town. It was a cool, dry day with the temperature around 30 degrees at the Wynne High School where the 8 AM start of the marathon took place. We wound through the streets of Wynne and up a half-mile hill as the course left town. From here the route was an out and back with rolling hills through rural Arkansas. Crowley Ridge lay on the west and the Mississippi Delta on the east. The aid stations showed up about every mile with everything a runner could need, from bananas, to Gatorade, to water, to Vaseline. The helpful volunteers always added a touch of Southern hospitality. The temperature rose to the mid 50s, with the sun shining as the race went on. I finished the first half in just under two hours, which was a good feeling. We made our way back to Wynne and a final lap around the high school track to the finish line. I completed my 36th state marathon in 4 hours and 17 minutes, my best time in five years. The average finish time was 4 hours and 29 minutes. I was 72nd out of 152 finishers.

On the way home I stopped at Cahokia, the ancient city of about 20,000 that seems to have disappeared around 1400 AD. I climbed the 92-foot Monks Mound, where the Chieftain lived with his direct connection to his brother the sun. I could get a good view across the state line to see the St. Louis Arch. After such a special marathon, I could almost feel like I belonged up there. Then I climbed back down to get in line at a McDonald's for a Caesar's Salad and realized I'm only one of three hundred million.

The ancient city of Cahokia's Monks Mound where the ruler
of the city lived

View of St. Louis across the Mississippi River from the
top of Cahokia's Monks Mound

King's Mountain Marathon

King's Mountain State Park, South Carolina

In early April of 2011, Lon and I took three days to drive down to the North Carolina and South Carolina border from Cable for the King's Mountain Marathon. Along the way we stopped at Greeneville, Tennessee, the home of our seventeenth President, Andrew Johnson. He had a hard act to follow, replacing Abraham Lincoln when he was shot. He was even impeached for firing Edward Stanton, Secretary of War. Andrew Johnson had humble beginnings as a runaway tailor's apprentice who never had formal education. He was an independent sort who made the statement, "It's a poor mind that can only think of one way to spell a word."

We met Jim and Diana Heinz in Gaffney, South Carolina. Jim took us to get our race packets and we all enjoyed our pre-marathon pasta dinner at Olive Garden.

Saturday morning was sunny and 62 degrees for the 8 AM start of the King's Mountain Marathon in the campground of King's Mountain State Park. The race started with an out and back in the campground before heading out on the park road. This road was curvy and hilly, not rolling hills but steep, long hills. Some runners provided their own support teams because the aid stations were four miles apart. The shade of trees that lined the route helped us along as the temperature rose to 84 degrees by afternoon. From the pavement of the park road, we went off on a dirt road for a couple of miles before running on a highway with about a one-foot shoulder and the always-present traffic. An occasional peach orchard and horse pasture cut into the forests along the course.

Finally we made our way back to the campground in the state park and the finish line. It was a tough marathon with very little level ground and high temperatures. I finished in 4 hours and 25 minutes. There were 65 finishers and I was 16th. I was second among the 50 – 59 age group, for which I was presented a glass mug. The average finish time was 5 hours and 3 minutes, telling us it was a tough marathon or we were a bunch of slow runners. Lon was twenty minutes behind me and Jim finished in a little over seven hours.

After the race Lon and I visited the neighboring King's Mountain National Battlefield. This Revolutionary War battle took place between American rebel militia and American Tory militia. Americans for freedom fought Americans for English rule. The rebel militia won the day by taking the Tories by surprise on top of the mountain. The Tories tried several bayonet charges but the accuracy of the long rifle couldn't be matched.

That evening we all ate a steak dinner before heading home. I had completed my 37th state marathon.

Kentucky Derby Marathon

Louisville, Kentucky

Henry Clay and his buddies organized horse racing in Kentucky as early as 1809, when they reorganized the Lexington Jockey Club. Many towns in Kentucky had a race street just off of Main Street where they could test their thoroughbreds' speed. In 1875 Louisville took horse racing a step further with the start of the Kentucky Derby at Churchill Downs. Today the winner among the three-year-old thoroughbreds gets just under one and a half million dollars for crossing the finish line first on the one and a quarter mile dirt track in front of up to 150,000 spectators. The race takes about two minutes. The winner is also draped in a blanket of 554 roses, giving the event the name, "The Run for the Roses."

"Of all human powers operating on the affairs of mankind, none is greater than that of competition," according to Henry Clay.

Competition in horse racing or competition in running a marathon, the Kentucky Derby Marathon brings both together.

Race day, April 30 of 2011, was sunny and 50 degrees at the start in downtown Louisville. There were about 11,000 runners in the half and full marathons together. The half had the full outnumbered by almost ten to one. The first part of the race was crowded as we ran through the streets of Louisville and out toward Churchill Downs at about mile eight. We ran through the grand stands, under the track and infield, and out the other side. The half marathoners left us at this point as we ran on Southern Parkway to Iroquois Park and the long, grinding hills that brought us to the halfway point. We left the park on the same Parkway and stayed on it until mile 17 where we had to start dodging slow half marathoners on the city streets. The temperature rose to about 70 but the route offered a lot of shade, which helped. At about mile 23, a backbreaker hill just wouldn't quit. My legs were stiffening up before this hill came up. Once over the top, we had a downhill grade on Main Street to the finish line. I definitely felt like two marathons in three weeks were too much. I finished in 4 hours and 42 minutes. That placed me at 998th out of 1,557 marathon finishers. Kentucky was my 38th state marathon.

A cool, damp Bar Harbor Marathon morning

The Maine coastline bordering some of the race

Mount Desert Island Marathon

Bar Harbor, Maine

The Mount Desert Marathon is described as the most scenic in America. I don't think that is a fair statement. Every marathon in a natural area has its own scenic beauty. Which one is most scenic is up to the beholder. One thing is for sure; any rural marathon is going to be more scenic than an urban marathon. What God creates offers much more than what man creates.

After flying into Boston, Denise and I drove up to Bar Harbor, Maine, on a cool, rainy Friday evening in October of 2011. We found a family style restaurant in Bar Harbor and had, what else, seafood.

The next morning Denise and I ran a 1.8-mile fun run through Bar Harbor. As part of the event, we were offered a breakfast buffet that included all those good tasting foods that probably aren't the best for someone running a marathon the next day. One of the runners at the table where we sat was talking about doing a marathon in Antarctica. Besides cold temperatures, he said if the weather was too bad, runners would have to run laps around the perimeter of the ship to get in their marathon. I had to ask how much for the trip and the answer was $10,000. That would be an expensive gamble, in my book.

That afternoon we explored Mount Desert Island, home to Acadia National Park and the racecourse. The island got its name in 1604 when Samuel de Champlain damaged his ship on rocks off shore. He was able to get to shore for materials to repair his ship, and named the island. It is a special place where ancient rock formations peek out of the fall leaf color show and contrast with evergreens, while the Atlantic Ocean crashes on shore among small New England villages.

Sunday morning, October 16 was race day. The 8 AM start in downtown Bar Harbor was cloudy and cool (upper 40s), with a few raindrops. This was a town for the super rich until 1947. The Vanderbilts, Morgans, and Astors all had homes here. Nelson Rockefeller, John D. Rockefeller's grandson, was born here. In 1947 drought hit the area. A cranberry bog fire broke out and expanded to include most of the eastern half of Mount Desert Island, including 67 homes on Millionaire Row. Downtown Bar Harbor escaped the fire. The race left downtown on a one-mile decline before the first hill, putting us in the shadow of Cadillac Mountain, the tallest mountain on the eastern shore of the United States at 1,532 feet. It got its name from an explorer who was the founder of Detroit, Michigan. From here we headed downhill toward the ragged cliffs of the island, as the Atlantic Ocean crashed on shore at such features as Thunder Hole, which has spray and sound to match its name. A strong headwind to side wind was our constant companion as we passed through the villages of Seal Harbor and Northeast Harbor where the only fjord on the Atlantic Ocean begins. Granite cliffs run right down to Sommes Sound. At mile twenty we passed through the village of Sommesville, which was founded by the Sommes family in 1761, making it the oldest village on the island. This family was asked by the Massachusetts governor to start some industry in the area. The Sommes took up fishing, shipbuilding, logging, and rock quarrying. They became the wealthiest family on the island. You can still feel that early New England lifestyle as you pass through the village.

From miles twenty to twenty-five we had an uphill grind. We heard our names as we passed through aid stations because our names were on our race bibs, which was a nice personal touch. Mile 25 was the high point on the course before we descended into Southwest Harbor and the finish line.

I was 385th out of 924 finishers in a time of 4 hours and 23 minutes on this hilly, wind-blown course. The average finish time was 4 hours and 50 minutes. I had my 39th state marathon.

My finish at the Mount Desert Marathon at Southwest. Harbor

Rehoboth Beach Marathon

Rehoboth Beach, Delaware

In December of 2011 I drove to Delaware, the trip taking me in and out of winter. When I got into the high country of Pennsylvania there was snow. I visited Fort Necessity, where young militia General George Washington more or less started the French and Indian War. He signed a paper without knowing its meaning, which said he was responsible for the death and mutilation of noncombatant French soldiers at the hands of our Indian allies under his command. I wonder if he took his own advice. It is better to offer no excuse than a bad one.

I crossed the Chesapeake Bay into Delaware and found Rehoboth Beach with some effort. It was time to pick up my race bib, and I took a walk on the boardwalk with the Atlantic Ocean on one side and shops on the other. A few were even open in December.

Rehoboth is a Biblical name. The town got its start in 1873 as the location of a Methodist Camp Ministry. Settlers too far from each other to support a church, came together and camped out for a few days to listen to a preacher, sing hymns, and socialize. Today Rehoboth Beach is a playground for Washington D.C.

The next morning, Saturday, December 10th I got up at 5:30 AM to arrive at the start of the marathon on the ocean side of downtown. It was just getting light at the 30 something degree, 7 AM start. The organizers didn't seem ready for the start, with port-a-potties showing up late and local restaurants not aware of the marathon start area or time.

The race began with a six mile out and back through Rehoboth and north along the shoreline. I was keeping a nine-minute-a-mile pace, but the mile markers were not accurate. Miles seven through ten went through the woods on Breakwater Trail. This is where my guts started to cease up and my time slowed down. Once we left the woods, a fifteen to twenty mile per hour wind also made its presence known and it wasn't helpful. We ran along a highway into the town of Lewes, Delaware, which is the oldest town (1662) in Delaware, our first state of the Union.

From the halfway point we ran through Cape Henlopen State Park with sand dunes and shoreline beaches. I was definitely feeling sharp pain in my stomach and back as we headed back toward Rehoboth. Breaking five hours started looking like a dream. I tried walking a little but had a hard time keeping my balance. The paramedics driving by once again seemed like vultures waiting for me to give it up.

By mile nineteen the wind was so strong off the ocean in the open areas, it felt like it could take you off your feet, especially how I was feeling. I looked at my watch and now I hoped to finish the last seven miles in two hours to make the six-hour cut off. I walked, shuffled, and watched other runners go by, but I made it to the finish line in 5 hours and 53 minutes. There were still 37 of the 637 finishers behind me. It wasn't what I hoped for, but I completed my 40th state marathon.

The Madonna Ranch and race headquarters with Bishop Peak in the background

Finishing the San Luis Obispo Marathon with the Mission de Tolosa in the inset

San Luis Obispo Marathon

San Luis Obispo, California

During the 1930s depression Will Rogers claimed, "When the Oakies left Oklahoma for California, it raised the I.Q. of both states." We know that statement isn't true but when one place is heard from too much, a claim like this kind of puts everyone on an even playing field again. It is kind of like what we deal with up North. We all know there are a lot of good people in Minnesota, but almost every time someone does something stupid on the road around here, you look at the license plate and it says Minnesota.

In April of 2012, we put opinions in their place and ran a marathon in California. Denise and I flew into Las Vegas, where Jim and Diana Heinz were good enough to drive us through the desert and over the southern tail of the Sierra Nevada Mountains into San Luis Obispo. A town of about 50,000, it lies somewhere between San Francisco and Los Angeles.

On Saturday, April 22, we all drove down to the Madonna Inn and Ranch, where the race would finish and race packet pickup was located. The ranch is located at the base of grassy Bishop Peak. At 1,546 feet, it is the tallest of the Nine Sisters Peaks in the California Coastal Range.

Sunday was race day, so Jim and I walked from the motel to the race start at the high school. Cloudy and misting the sky just started to lighten for the 6 AM marathon start. The temperature was probably in the upper 50s and didn't move much through the race. Jim was doing the half marathon with about two thousand other runners.

In the first mile or so of the marathon, we passed the Mission de Tolosa, where San Luis Obispo got its start. Father Junipero Serra started the mission in 1772, making San Luis Obispo one of the oldest towns in California. The earliest settlers faced starvation, so a hunting party was sent out in what is known as the Valley of the Bears. They came back with 25 mules packed with dried bear meat to save the Spanish mission.

About five miles into the race, the course took us out of town and into the continuous hills of the Edna Valley. We passed four vineyards, seven wineries, and dairy farms with cows mooing to welcome us or tell us to keep it moving. At the twelve and a half mile mark we made a turn around and headed back toward town with a detour that took us for about six miles on Corbett Canyon Road. The hills remained and the day continued to be cool and cloudy.

At mile 24 we were back in town, crossing the Jennifer Street Bridge which started and ended with steel and concrete switchbacks to get us above Highway 101. On the other side, a bike path took us up and over one more hill leading into Madonna Ranch with a white wooden fence on both sides. When I was within a quarter of a mile from the finish, the four-hour thirty-minute pacer passed by, but he had only two runners with him. Then I saw Denise standing on the fence, encouraging me on as I finished in 4 hours and 29 minutes. The average finish time was 4 hours and 39 minutes. I was 342nd out of 663 marathon finishers. My 41st state marathon was complete.

When we got back to Las Vegas, Jim, a couple of his friends, and I took an eleven-mile kayak trip on the Colorado River from Hoover Dam to Willow Creek Campground. Along the way we stopped to investigate a cave that had knee-deep hot spring water in it. The cave became considerably warmer as we waded deeper in the cave. While traveling down the river, we stopped again at a hot springs waterfall that we used for a warm shower. Another stop featured hot spring pools that served for a sauna. It was a good way to recover from the marathon before heading home.

Jim and I discuss the warm waterfalls that run into the Colorado River.

Mad Marathon

Waitsfield, Vermont

In July of 2012, Lon and I boarded an airplane in Minneapolis and flew to Logan Airport in Boston, where we were to meet Jim Heinz and head north to Vermont for the Mad Marathon. The only problem was, we were a bunch of low-tech guys in a high-tech world, trying to use cell phones to make our connection. I ended up calling Denise back in Wisconsin to contact Jim Heinz and tell him we were in the same airport, before I threw the little technological wonder across the airport. With Denise's help, we found Jim, got our Black Ford Fusion rental, and headed north to Montpelier, Vermont.

The next day we drove to Waitsfield, founded in 1789 by General Benjamin Wait. He fought in the French and Indian War before joining Ethan Allen and the Green Mountain Boys in the Revolutionary War. The visitor center is the first building he put up.

The village green was the center of activity on this Saturday morning with a farmer's market, crafts, and the race expo where we picked up our race packets. Waitsfield is one of those places where nature dominates the landscape and people from Boston and New York work fifty weeks so they can spend two weeks here. They say it isn't quite heaven but you're almost there. That evening we had our pasta dinner at the New England style Waitsfield Inn.

Sunday morning, July 8, we drove back to Waitsfield from Montpelier for the 7 AM marathon start on Highway 100, which goes right through the middle of town. It was a sunny, mid-60s New England morning. We started the marathon by running through town on the highway and turned off on East Warren Rd., where we all had to fit through a narrow covered bridge that took us over the Mad River. This is where we left town and the hills started. I even walked a little on the top of the first hill because I knew many more hills were ahead. I didn't want to burn out on my second attempt at a Vermont marathon after I couldn't make the cut-off in the Jay Mountain Ultramarathon I spoke of earlier.

We came to a dirt road heading out to mile six and a turn around at Carpenter Farm. There were several farms along the course. Some have been in the family for generations and others are owned by

111

relatively newcomers looking for a better life than a city can offer. They have figured out, like Ben Franklin had, "Money has never made man happy nor will it, there is nothing in its nature to produce happiness. The more of it one has the more one wants." The Bible was probably Ben's source for that truth.

The hilltops kept coming with those "million dollar" views of the Green Mountains. This combination gave the race the nickname, "beauty and the beast."

The back roads kept coming too, and some were dirt. A head wind kicked up to cool the low 70s temperature. The aid stations always had water and Gatorade with energy gels in the second half and one station even offered watermelon. That was a nice touch. The last nine miles started a downhill trend back down to the Mad River Valley. We went back under the same covered bridge where we started the race, but this time it wasn't crowded. The course took us back up Highway 100 to the town green, where organizer Dori Ingalls stood to greet each finisher of the marathon. I finished in 4 hours and 43 minutes, which was good for 158th out of 271 finishers. Lon was ahead of me by 16 minutes and was the 124th finisher. Jim Heinz finished in 5 hours and 36 minutes and was the 242nd finisher. The average finish time was 4 hours and 35 minutes. I finally had my Vermont marathon and my 42nd state marathon. After the race we headed up to Waterbury for ice cream at Ben and Jerry's.

Gruene, TX above the Guadalupe River Valley and the Chosen Marathon. I'm holding my age class award—a record.

The Chosen Marathon

New Braunfels, Texas

In October, 2012, Denise and I flew into San Antonio, Texas, around noon. We headed north 35 miles to New Braunfels in our rental car. We stopped for lunch at an IHOP and the waiter told us that New Braunfels was his home and it had great German people who knew how to barbecue. Our next stop was The Natural Bridge Wildlife Ranch with 40 species of animals from six continents, mostly running wild on a four-mile circle drive. We even experienced an ostrich sticking his head in the car window. It made you think of what Noah was up against, getting the animals into the ark.

After checking into our motel, Denise and I drove to the small historic town of Gruene, where the marathon would start and finish. Henry Gruene, who had a 6,000-acre cotton farm in the 1870s and several sharecroppers, started the town. He built a general store and a dance hall, as a small town sprang up. In 1910 the boll weevil wiped out the cotton and the town became a ghost town before the buildings were rejuvenated in the 1970s and the town became a tourist center with the dance hall still providing entertainment. We enjoyed a pasta dinner at one of the establishments as the 87-degree sun started easing toward the end of the day.

Friday was a different world. The temperature was in the fifties, windy, and with a little rain. We headed for LBJ's ranch near Johnson City, set in the Texas Hill Country. You can see the ranch as the Johnsons left it; clothes, kitchen utensils, and three TVs in view of the dining room table so President Johnson could call any newscaster who disrespected him on the 6 PM news on the spot, from a phone he had mounted under the table. He also had an outdoor pool installed in the backyard on doctor's orders to exercise, so he bought an inflatable raft and floated around.

Saturday morning started early as we headed back to Gruene and the Rockin R Hotel for the 7:15 AM start of the Chosen Marathon. They had coffee available at the start, which meant nothing to me, but Denise liked it. It was still before sunup, cloudy, in the upper 40s, with a stiff north wind. The race took off after a prayer by the organizer's pastor, in the parking lot of the hotel. The first mile was uphill, followed by a couple of rolling miles before a three-quarter mile downhill to the Guadalupe River Valley. At that point the course took the road upstream along the river with rock outcroppings, rolling hills, and trees along the road. We had four river crossings by the halfway turn around. I made it there in 1 hour and 57 minutes, which made me feel great. The aid stations showed up about every mile with friendly people shouting, "how you doing brother?"

Downstream meant downhill for the second half, but rolling hills evened things out. At mile 22 we headed out of the river valley and up that three-quarter mile hill. I still ran the whole thing, but many didn't. I was still feeling good on this cool day. The sun was coming out and the wind was always there but manageable. The last mile was downhill and appreciated. I finished my 43rd state marathon in 4 hours and 6 minutes, which made a pretty special day that would only get better. The course was even one-tenth of a mile long. I was 60th out of 176 marathon finishers, first in my class, and I set a course record in the 60+ age group. The second place finisher came in at 4 hours and 28 minutes. The previous two years (this was the marathon's 3rd year), the winners finished in 4 hours and 40 minutes and 5 hours and 28 minutes. This was my first time to set a record. It would last only one year, but this would always be my record. The only downside was, at the awards ceremony I had to ask for my medal; I guess they never thought anyone 60+ would be in yet.

A guy named Josh helped us find our way around the race area the day before. He'd lived in Minneapolis and worked at 3M. At the finish he was there to help direct runners. He remembered me from the day before as he directed me to the finish, and he shouted, "Way to go Mr. Anderson," with tears in his eyes. A marathon can be emotional.

Back in San Antonio we stayed at the Crocket Hotel, LBJ's favorite. We toured the Alamo across the street. At the time of the battle the fort was bigger and the mission didn't have the fancy top it has today. Our guide said Santa Anna's 1,800 troops sneaked up on the 189 defenders who were awakened by, "Viva La Mexico." An hour later they were all dead in the early morning dawn after fighting for Texan Independence. The next morning Denise and I left at 4 AM for our flight home knowing we were part of a marathon that provided adoptive parents of orphans with $180,000.

Rocket City Marathon

Huntsville, Alabama

Will Rogers once said, "Even if you're on the right track, you'll get run over if you just sit there."

I wasn't going to just sit there. I had just completed a 4:06 marathon on a challenging course and was out to run a 3 hour and 55 minute marathon so I would qualify for the Boston Marathon. It is the world's oldest marathon and one of few with a qualifying time. Getting in represents a standard of excellence to runners. Qualifying for Boston became my goal for the flat Rocket City Marathon.

In December of 2012, I headed south toward Huntsville, Alabama. I stopped at Dixon, Illinois to visit Ronald Reagan's hometown where he grew up. The town speaks of President Reagan in several sites. I toured his boyhood home, looked through a museum in his high school, and had my picture taken next to a statue of Ronald Reagan on a horse by the Rock River. He often said, "There is nothing better for the inside of a man than the outside of a horse."

The next day I drove through Nashville and stopped at Franklin, Tennessee, the location of the Battle of Franklin during the Civil War in November of 1864. It was the bloodiest five hours of the war, with much of it fought after dark. I visited the Carnton Plantation Mansion the next morning that served as a Confederate hospital to 300 wounded soldiers. Bloodstains can still be seen on the floor.

Later that day I found Huntsville's Holiday Inn and picked up my race packet. I also had a spaghetti dinner there with runner Bill Rodgers as the speaker. He said a 46-minute 10km. was doing pretty well for him at this point. I'm thinking I can do a 49-minute 10 km. so I must be doing okay, seeing as I'm in the same age bracket.

The next morning, Saturday of December 8, I went back to the Holiday Inn early with a game plan for the marathon. I was going to find the four-hour pacer, stay with him, and give it a little extra at the end to get my Boston Qualifier. I talked over race plans with a couple of other runners. The morning was humid, in the 60s, and cloudy. I didn't give the weather enough thought in my plan. The race started less than a block away at 8 AM. I found my pacer, a young lady with a red ballerina outfit, not what I expected. As the race took off, I had trouble finding her in the crowd of runners, even with her outfit. She seemed to speed up and slow down, not what I needed. By mile four the sweat was coming off my hat like rain. I started slowing down as the pacer moved away. I lost a lot of fluids in my effort to stay with the pacer and was in trouble. As the race progressed, the guys I had talked to about a plan for the race back in the hotel, ran by, one at a time, which was even more demoralizing. At mile ten through fourteen there was a long straight stretch and the sun came out.

My goals for the race were long gone, except to finish and get my 44th state. At mile twenty they were passing out salt tablets because of the heat and humidity, but I decided to try an Herbalife drink instead. I didn't notice much improvement. At times, even standing was a problem. I found a stride somewhere between a walk and jog to keep me going.

Near the finish, my mind went in a totally different direction. I hoped to get back to the Carter House, which was the Union Headquarters at the Battle of Franklin, before it closed for the day. It is amazing how the mind can change direction from a fast marathon time to a Civil War Battle. I didn't want to think about the disappointment of the day.

I did finish in 5 hours and 30 minutes, which placed me 1054th out of 1144 finishers. I got my 44th state marathon but it wasn't what I hoped for. I did get back to Franklin, Tennessee in time to see the Carter House and enjoy a good supper at Cracker Barrel. I guess John Bell Hood, the Confederate Commander at the Battle of Franklin, and I have something in common. We both overestimated our capabilities on a given day. My overestimation cost only a little pride but General Hood's cost 8,500 casualties.

Ocean Drive Marathon

Cape May, New Jersey

Lon and I flew into Baltimore and drove down to Washington D.C. on Thursday, March 21 of 2013. Saving dollars on flight tickets made the drive down to Washington worthwhile.

We hiked around the many monuments in our nation's capital. The Korean War Memorial stood out from the rest, with soldiers at eye level making their way through actual bushes. Very impressive. The U.S. Capitol building had a majestic presence. The White House disappointed me due to all the homeless people living in a field beyond the guarded fences—a poor statement of our world today.

On Friday we traveled to New Jersey, as did George Washington and his army over 200 years ago. Lon and I walked on the bridge over the Delaware River where General Washington and his army crossed in small boats in a sleet storm to surprise the Hessians the day after Christmas. The mission got behind schedule but Washington wanted to keep things upbeat. The formal, proper general even got a little coarse with his men as he took his turn to get on board a boat. He is said to have stepped over men and nudged his 300-pound Artillery Officer, Henry Knox with the toe of his boot, and pranked, "Shift that fat rear, Harry. But slowly, or you'll swamp the dang boat."

On our way down to Cape May we stopped at Cladwell, New Jersey on Saturday morning. There stood a typical, middle class, mid-nineteenth century home with a white picket fence, the birthplace of our 22nd and 24th president, Grover Cleveland. He was also the first president to be married for the first time while President and to a lady 27 years younger than himself. A piece of their wedding cake is still in the Cladwell home to see. The Baby Ruth candy bar is named after their first child, Ruth. Grover is said to have gained one hundred pounds in one year, definitely not a runner.

That afternoon Lon and I found the Congress Hall Hotel in Cape May and picked up our race packets. I discovered a church supper advertised in town, so we enjoyed good, homemade food at a good price with friendly, mostly elderly people.

Sunday morning meant a ten-mile drive back to Cape May for a thirty something degree 9 AM start of the Ocean Drive Marathon. I waited inside the warm hotel with many other runners for the start. It was a mostly sunny morning with a breeze but not as big of a headwind problem as in past years. The course took us north from Cape May, with the road close enough to see the ocean and nearby marshland when we weren't going through an Oceanside town. We had to cross five bridges on the course, which presented us with the only hills. I followed three ladies doing the ten-mile for the first part of the race, which helped make the wind a no factor.

At the seaside town of Wildwood, we ran on the boardwalk for miles nine and ten. Most of the shops were closed because of the off-season. I finished the first half of the marathon near the town of Angelsea in a time of 2 hours and 15 minutes. During the second half I was on my own most of the time. The ten-milers were gone and I was still feeling pretty strong. We passed through the seaside towns of Stone Harbor and Avalon with their ocean view condos, both built and being built. As the last six miles were coming to an end the clouds darkened, the wind strengthened, and the temperature started sinking. I made it to Sea Isle City and the finish line in 4 hours and 27 minutes, which gave me a negative split, finishing the second half three minutes faster than the first. Lon finished three minutes ahead of me. I felt hypothermia coming on, so I tried a little hot soup before making my way to the return bus. New Jersey was my 45th state marathon.

Cox Marathon

Providence, Rhode Island

On Wednesday, May 8, 2013 I flew into Baltimore. Jim Heinz picked me up at the airport. We drove down to Manassas Battlefield in Virginia. It rained while we discussed with a park volunteer how a wounded Wisconsin Civil War soldier survived one week on the battlefield before being rescued just outside the window of the park building where we were standing. The next day we visited the U.S. Capitol and sat in on the House of Representatives in action. It looked like mass confusion. Congressmen talked to each other all over the room and the gavel pounded on the podium to get everyone's attention, with little result. Mark Twain's advice, "It is better to remain silent and be thought a fool than to open one's mouth and remove all doubt," seemed to be ignored by them.

On Friday, we drove north to Massachusetts. We traveled right through New York City with two kayaks on the top of Jim's diesel pickup. Crossing the George Washington Bridge was interesting, and cost $13 to cross the Hudson River.

Saturday we drove to downtown Providence, looked through the expo, and picked up our race packets at the Omni Hotel.

Sunday morning started early. Jim wanted to make sure we got a good parking spot for his large diesel pickup, so we got up at 3 AM. Driving to downtown Providence, then found a spot and tried to sleep a little before walking over to the start area. It rained and the start was delayed a bit, with a few showers making things interesting. The race was to start at 7:30 AM with a great deal of security around. The Boston tragedy was still on everyone's mind. The race started out kind of cool at about 58 degrees, but the humidity made it feel warm in a hurry as the race got going.

The temperature rose to about 70 degrees during the race. The start and finish bordered a park where pre-and post-race activities centered. There were some hills; I remember an abrupt uphill at about mile 23. Quite a bit of bike trail, with skyscrapers sticking above the trees, offered a nice change from city streets. Many mile markers were off the mark, making pacing difficult. The race ended up being between a quarter and half mile too long. Some runners trying to qualify for Boston were very upset because they lost their qualifier by a minute or two, due to the course not being measured correctly. The water stops were sufficient with all the energy gels you could want.

I started out fairly well with a half marathon time of 2 hours and 11 minutes, but I wasn't to have a good day. It may have been motion sickness catching up with me, getting up at 3 AM, humidity, or just plain not a good day. The second half went very slowly, especially when the sun came out. I finished in 4 hours and 56 minutes. Jim came in a little over a half hour latter. They had cold pizza at the finish, not my favorite.

I did get my 46th state marathon, 1022 out of 1242 finishers.

Finish line of the Hartford Marathon

Hartford Marathon

Hartford, Connecticut

At five-thirty AM, my brother Bryan drove me to the airport to make a 7 AM flight to Hartford, Connecticut. I sat by a guy headed for New Haven, Connecticut, to support his son in his minor league effort in hockey. We arrived in Hartford and I was on the city bus at eleven. Bus fare cost $1.30, much better than the $50 taxicabs wanted. I checked in at the Ramada, ate lunch at a Subway (always a 6" meatball sub), and hiked to Samuel Clemens's house.

Clemens, (Mark Twain) owned a 3-story home with an indoor garden. It was built to impress and does. It's a good thing his wife had money to afford the high living and entertaining they did. They invited everyone over who was "someone," from General Grant to JP Morgan. After dinner the men would go to the third floor and Sam's billiard room to drink, smoke, tell stories, and even play billiards. As Mark Twain said, "Go to Heaven for the climate, Hell for the company." That's where he wrote Huckleberry Finn and Tom Sawyer. Samuel Clemens knew, "Don't go around saying the world owes you a living. The world owes you nothing. It was here first."

On the way back downtown, I looked over the marathon finish area at Bushnell Park and the landmark arch. I had a pasta feast with many other runners at the Hartford Club, a nice place.

Marathon morning, October 12, 2013,I had a muffin and tea at Dunkin' Donuts. I helped fill in some policemen about the marathon. They couldn't believe we paid to do it. Their main concern was, the event made an early start to their day. So I looked around the start area next to the capitol, deciding it was time to check in. I was shocked to see the line. It stretched down to the street, across the road, and up the stairs on the building across the street. I made it to the start line in time to hear a police officer sing the national anthem, a United Church of Christ pastor offer an extended well-thought-out prayer, and some dancers performing to "Sweet Caroline."

The gun fired and 13,000 half and full marathon runners took off. It took me two minutes to get to the start line and nine minutes for everyone to get going. The first half of the race was cool, shaded by office buildings. The Ucan shake seemed to work quite well to give me energy. It took me 2 hrs. and 8 min. for the first 13 miles. The second half warmed up with the sun to about 70 degrees and it felt humid to me. There was music about every mile that included some Hari Krisnas who were passing out water. I was losing my momentum, starting to feel dizzy, and slowing down. The last 6 miles took over an hour and a half as we headed downtown on Asylum Avenue toward the arch at Bushnell Park. I finished in 5 hrs. and 5 minutes but at least I finished. There were about 500 runners behind me out of 2,700 finishers. I had my 47th state marathon.

After I finished, clouds cooled things down. The space blanket felt good. My medal was classy. Food for the runners was great—tomato soup, grilled cheese sandwiches, apple crisp, and chocolate milk.

I walked back past the oldest church in Hartford and sat down for a bit. The church dates back to 1632 and Thomas Hooker, who also started the colony. Next to the church is a cemetery, with markers going back to 1642. There was some construction next door and they placed a port-a-potty right next to some of the markers; others lay on a pallet like lumber. I thought the respect for the dead was lacking.

The next morning, my first concern was figuring out bus connections to the airport. I asked at the hotel. They said look on their computer. No luck. I asked at Dunkin Donuts. A guy there said ask a supervisor in a green vest. I asked the bus driver. He said "on the hour." I decided at 8 AM I had time to visit the 250-year-old Christ Church Cathedral. It was a huge, impressive building with a congregation of only 10 and four people officiating the service. I decided that I still had time to go to the 380-year-old First Church of Christ. They were holding a service of remembrance to honor the ancient cemetery next to it. As part of the service, they included the oldest continuously active military unit in the United States. The unit's original job was to protect the governor. After, I tried to catch the bus. It had left a minute earlier. I found one of those green vested supervisors. She told me to get in the back seat of her car and she'd catch the bus. When that failed, she took me all 15 miles to the airport. I tried to pay her, but she wouldn't even take bus fare. I told her I'd write the company to tell them what she did. That was good with her. I followed through on my end of the bargain and I received a note of appreciation.

"There are basically two types of people. People who accomplish things, and people who claim to have accomplished things. The first group is less crowded."
Mark Twain

Built in 1874, Mark Twain's home definitely
speaks of accomplishment.

First Church of Christ founded in 1632, the service
including the oldest continuously active military unit, and
the ancient cemetery next door

Myles Standish Marathon

Plymouth, Massachusetts

Friday, November 15, 2013, started with a call from Lora, the secretary at LCO School near Hayward, Wisconsin. They wanted me to teach high school history. I was planning to head to the Twin Cities that afternoon and take the early flight to Boston the next morning. Things change and change can be good, so I went to LCO first. Being an emergency, I was pretty much on my own. The kids can be a tough crowd, especially to a sub, but I like history and the classes went fine. I made my way down to Minneapolis after school.

The next morning, the plane ride to Boston was great with only 40 passengers, plenty of room to stretch out. When I picked up my rental car, I let myself get talked into buying extra insurance.

I headed down to Plymouth, checked into the Radisson, and got my race packet. We had a dialect problem there. They couldn't find my race number. They were going to have me sign up again when they discovered I was saying Anderson and not Henderson. My New England accent isn't there yet. I then headed to Plimouth Plantation Historical Park to see how things went in 1627 for the Wampanoag and pilgrim villagers. The Wampanoag were burning and digging out the inside of a white pine log to make a dugout canoe. The English villagers were busy getting their firewood in for the night, but they don't let it burn all night because they can't trust their thatched roofs.

That night I ate at Friendly's, a nice restaurant where seniors are treated well, including ten percent off, plus a free ice cream sundae. Next morning started early with a bus from Plymouth High School to the hills of Myles Standish State Forest. We hiked about a mile back on the same road to the start. The race was delayed and the traffic kept coming both ways. It was a cool morning, in the 40s with very little sun. Finally everyone arrived at the start. We started on a downhill, then back up, winding through the forest on a hilly course. I was going well with an 8 minute, 37 second first mile. About mile ten my time slowed. Traffic was bad, cars showing little respect for runners and in places we had only a foot or two to work with along a raised curb. I had a 2 hour, 9 minute first half. Then, for the second marathon in a row, "the wall" took over. The hills became a real obstacle. The dirt road for two miles was a welcome change of pace, but once we got back in town I was barely hanging on. The last hill leading up to the school loomed ahead. I finished in 5 hours and 21minutes, 251st out of 263 finishers, which doesn't set well but it was the best I could do that day. This was my 48th state.

I thought, for my next marathon, I'm going to take some advice from Abe Lincoln, "Give me six hours to chop down a tree and I will spend the first four sharpening the axe." I'm going to us those "four hours" to figure out what I can do differently. Maybe the Lyme's disease from last summer is still having lingering effects.

When I recovered, I went back out to the same plantation and attended 1627 church. The elder chosen as pastor of the pilgrims told us Sundays were totally spent at church. Winter was a challenge because of no fire in the church. After church I got into a discussion with a "pilgrim" named Master Hopkins. He didn't think much of having to go to church or the Governor putting him in stocks for a sword fight with another villager. These people live and speak the 1600s. They even study to do the job. If you ask a question that isn't time-oriented they just look confused.

That Monday afternoon, I made my way through Boston, Brookline in particular, and found John Kennedy's birthplace. It struck me that Rose Kennedy had the place refurnished as it was when the kids were growing up. She gave the kids strict time regimens. They had only so much time to play, wash, read, and so on. She hired a cook and one other servant so the kitchen was a bit of mystery to her. Later, I went to the JFK Library, which replayed his presidency in vivid detail.

Back in Plymouth, I went to Friendly's one more time before heading to Boston and the airport. I found Boston-style rush hour with the "breakdown lane" traffic going 60-70 MPH. I don't know what would have happened if there had been a breakdown. It took me several hours to cover the 40+ miles to the airport.

Time to go back home to the simpler life in the North woods of Wisconsin where what should be is most of the time. I agree with Pete Seeger on this one, "Any darn fool can make something complex; it takes a genius to make something simple."

New Orleans Marathon

New Orleans, Louisiana

Denise and I landed in New Orleans Thursday, January 30, 2014, a sunny day in the 60s, quite a change from the single digits in Cable. We found the city bus to get us downtown. A wiry, gray-haired guy working information directed us to a statue of Louis Armstrong to find the city bus downtown. He saw my Grandfather Mountain Marathon shirt and asked if they still had the Scottish Clans and the caber throw. I learned he had completed the 50 states marathons.

Our big black bus driver got a kick out of us small town folks. Every time I asked a question, he'd reply, "How big is Cable?" The answer was always about 250. We finally figured out how to put our $4 fare in the very particular money machine. Moving now, I held onto Denise while she put the dollars in. The driver said that he'd never seen it done that way. He dropped us a block from the Holiday Inn – Superdome, our hotel. Cindi, the connoisseur at the hotel, helped us find the Acme Oyster House, a great place to eat.

After meeting with Cindi, we headed to the 17th floor of the hotel to find our room. I noticed my little bag with my camera and prescription sunglasses was missing. Denise figured she left it on the city bus. We headed back down to the lobby. Cindi phoned the bus company. They told us to meet the bus on its next time around on his route. We hoped no one took the bag and that the bus driver would remember us. When the bus came, I rushed out to meet it. The driver had our bag on the dash and he recognized this small-town guy right away. I thanked him and I'm sure I had a big smile. God answers prayer.

Denise and I headed to the Acme Oyster House off Bourbon Street. We had a sampler platter for two with fried fish, shrimp, oysters, sweet potato fries, jambalaya, and bread pudding with whiskey sauce New Orleans style. Bourbon Street was coming to life on our way back to the hotel. People were made up as statues in weird poses. One guy was a yellow racecar. Another had made a ladder that he was climbing. I'm not sure where he was going with that.

The next morning we went to Honey Island Swamp, looking for gators. Our guide, Sonny, took us on an open boat at a pretty good clip on the Pearl River to an inlet where wildlife would be easier to see. It was cool, with ice on the base of some cypress trees. We ended up seeing only a couple of friendly raccoons that liked marshmallows. The gators stayed at the bottom of the river and only surfaced once every 8 to 10 hours. Gators can live 70 years. They grow about one-and-a-half feet a year when they are young. Back at the company store, I held one of the little guys. We stopped at Indian Village on the east side of the Pearl River. It's the sort of place you don't go unless invited. The homes sit right on the river, most built with a lot of tin. They've been there for some time. Upkeep was not an issue. Everyone was out hunting, fishing, trapping, or at school when we were there so it was safe to visit. One sign said, Go Away, Trespassers will be Violated. To go to school, kids get in a boat, cross the river to the west side, and get on a bus at the boat landing

That afternoon, on the Creole Queen paddlewheel, we traveled upriver five miles on the Mississippi to the Battlefield of Chalmette, where Andrew Jackson beat the British in the final battle of the War of 1812.

In the evening, we had pasta at Frank's in the French Quarter, then walked back through Bourbon Street. I took pictures of the Friday night-lights. Saturday morning, Cajun Encounters picked us up again to go to Oak Alley and Laura sugar cane plantations. Oak Alley is known for its 28 oaks lining the entry to the mansion. The Creole plantation called Laura followed Creole tradition of the plantation, being handed down to the smartest, not necessarily the oldest child, even handing it over to a girl (Laura). We saw oranges and grapefruit along with the sugarcane. These plantation owners usually owned a second home in New Orleans for the off-season and the celebration of Mardi Gras.

The next morning, Sunday February 2 came fast. The Weather Channel said it was 63 degrees and 100% humidity at 6 AM. Denise and I walked the eight blocks to the start area of the marathon. A photographer with the marathon took our picture, then I found a port-a-potty, tried out my legs, and had a banana with water. It was time to find corral 9. They sent out a corral every two minutes with about a thousand marathoners and half marathoners in each corral. There were about 16,000 runners. 12,000 were half marathoners. After a Baptist choir member sang the national anthem, the horn went off every two minutes until they got to corral number 9. We reached the start line and were off. I had to make my way through constant runners for the first 12 and half miles. Runners who go a mile, then walk a minute can really get in the way, especially when coupled with old streets full of cracks, bumps, and holes. The fog and occasional mist made my new prescription sunglasses almost impossible to see through. I couldn't even see the time on my watch. Somehow I managed to keep a 10-minute mile pace through the first half of the marathon, despite the heavy air that seemed to sit in the trees lining St. Charles Street on the out and back. Sweat just rolled off. By mile 10, we were down in the French Quarter and the French Market, where Denise had spent some time looking but not buying the day before. I spotted a port-a-potty without a line so I stopped. Back in the race I felt better as we headed up to City Park where we would lose the half marathoners and there would be space to run my own race. I finished the first half in 2 hours and 11 minutes. The crowds, old streets, and humidity made that an accomplishment. The last half was an L-shaped out-and-back along Lake Pontchartrain. A head-to-cross-wind off the lake actually put a chill in the air in places. The only hills of any kind were overpasses in this part of the race. It stayed cloudy all day but the rain and fog went away so I started to see through my glasses. There was music along the route quite often, some of it live and some recorded. The food stations were well stocked and the volunteers well meaning, even if their comments weren't always on the mark. They would get the mile markers wrong or they would say don't quit now. One guy was hollering out "water here" and I was asking for water, but he didn't get it. Finally I shouted, "I need water!"

I finished in 4 hours and 53 minutes, my first wintertime marathon. One week before, I skied the Seeley Hills 18km Classic and one week after the marathon, the 26km Prebirkie cross-country ski race with temperatures around 0. I was 1740th out of 2749 finishers in the marathon. I had finished my 49th state marathon.

Denise met me at the finish line and told me she was told we would never make our flight because of traffic. We had a mile to cover to get to the shuttle, so I tried to run again. Another runner told me I was showing off. The first class shuttle bus got us back to the start area in good time. I asked a marathon volunteer which way to the Holiday Inn. Once we got past my mispronunciation of streets we were on our way with Denise in the lead. She reached the hotel first, got a cab, and asked for our bags. I was impressed. The cab driver was a good guy who even spoke English. He got us to the airport in time; I had time to change my sweaty running garb. The flight was late, so the pilot tried to skip refueling. Bad idea. We had to refuel in Peoria and we missed our transfer flight in Chicago. It took two requests to get on standby. We had to hope passengers from Orlando and Wichita didn't get across the airport terminal in time. They didn't and we made it to Minneapolis. We had to jump start our car before I could drive home. We got to Cable at a little after 1 AM. From a marathon in New Orleans, to a messed-up flight, to driving home, it made for a long day.

If I ever do the New Orleans Marathon again, I'll remember the Cajun method of getting ready; carbo-load on Jambalaya and crawfish, then eat powder-sugared beignets at Café du Monde.

Bourbon Street

Indian Village on the Pearl River

Original music in the French Quarter

The wet start of the New Orleans Marathon

The Harry Lundeberg School of Seamanship at Piney Point
over the Lower Potomac. This was the start and finish area of
the Lower Potomac Marathon

Two Marathons in Six Days

Lower Potomac and Rock-N-Roll Marathons

Chesapeake Bay and Washington D.C.

With 49 states completed, I thought it was time to have the Fifty States Club look at my marathons and make sure everything was in order. They found a problem. The Freedom Run would not be accepted as my Maryland marathon because it didn't start or finish in Maryland, although I ran about five miles through Antietam Battlefield in Maryland. The race started at Harpers Ferry, West Virginia, and ended in Shepherdstown, West Virginia. I didn't appreciate the technicality, but I was running in Washington DC in March of 2014 so I looked for a marathon in Maryland that was within a week. I found Piney Point. It would be the first time I would be doing two marathons in a week but I would try. It helped that I found a flight, car, and a decent motel for a week all for under $900.

Flying from Minneapolis to Washington DC was no problem. The weather changed from the teens and snow everywhere to 50s and a pile of snow here and there. I picked up my Nissan Versa with its smoke-covered smell that open windows seemed to cure. I tried following Map Quest directions to Fredericksburg but the road disappeared. I asked a mechanic under a car and got there just fine, except for a traffic jam on I-95. Two women in separate cars stood outside their cars in the middle lane talking on their phones while the rest of us crawled by with questioning looks.

I finally got to Fredericksburg, checked in to the Days Inn and went over to Perkins next door for noodles over chicken. When I returned to the motel, I fell asleep while waiting for Denise to call. In a little while, the motel clerk knocked on the door saying Denise was trying to get hold of me. I checked out the motel phone and found wires missing. Then I looked at the wall and there was a hole where the phone jack was supposed to go. I ended up using the motel clerk's phone, nice guy. I finally got to sleep. It didn't last long because I had to get up at 3:45 AM to leave at 4:15 for Piney Point, Maryland, and the Lower Potomac Marathon. Everyone I asked gave me different directions. I wanted to get going, in case I got a little bewildered along the way. I finally found a guy in a convenience store who worked by the 301 Bridge over the Potomac and into Maryland. I liked his directions and they got me to the Harry Lundeberg School of Seamanship in Piney Point where the marathon started. I felt like I deserved a medal for arriving 45 minutes before the 7:15 start. It was cool and cloudy, probably in the low 40s, so long handles under running shorts felt good. All 200 of us seemed to have difficulty finding the start. It ended up being along one of the exits from the school. As the morning sky started to lighten, we were off, heading out of town and over another Potomac River bridge. It represented one of the only hills on the first half of the marathon. It was a winding first half through Southern Pines. Traffic didn't exist. I found a comfortable pace and made it in 2 hours and 6 minutes for 13.1 miles. At times I had to ask about turn-offs because they weren't marked. The volunteers assumed we knew the route. Aid stations showed up about every two miles. The second half of the marathon was an out and back on a fairly well traveled highway with some longer hills. There was also a 10 to 15 MPH head wind for three or four miles. It was like fighting an uphill you can't see. A Korean lady passed me and said she enjoyed following my stride. A compliment appreciated. I like it quiet when I run, and the highway kind of kills that. To make things worse, at the last food station a Korean guy banged on a gong with enthusiasm. I got back to Harry's School of Seamanship in 4 hours and 39 minutes. I received a nice commemorative award for finishing third out of nine in my class. The marathon served a nice pasta buffet after the race in a school dining room with huge windows overlooking the Potomac River, which is really the Chesapeake Bay.

The next day, I visited Mount Vernon to get the rest of George Washington's story. It is definitely the most visited presidential home, and even on Monday morning I had to wait in line to get into the mansion. George's human side shows through as you learn about his estate. He liked to impress people. The road up to his home was built to give the visitors a glimpse of the grandeur of his plantation several times before you get there. I wonder what George would think of a museum, visitor center, and a food court in his honor. The food court hit me as a little much. It didn't look to me as if many people in that fast food area were thinking of George Washington.

During a daily memorial for George and Martha at their present resting place, it was brought out that when the Revolutionary War officers were going to march on the capital for their back pay George, showed up at their meeting and gave a speech telling them they were destroying everything they fought for. The speech didn't make as big an impact as he did when he took out his spectacles, showing the frailty that his service to the country had caused. There were few dry eyes in the room. Washington always put the country first.

Tuesday I went to Charles City to visit President John Tyler's home. As I drove southeast of Richmond, I stopped and asked three road construction workers where Charles City was. They told me I was in it, Charles City being a county, not a city. I arrived early so I looked at Shirley Plantation, which had been established in 1613. It was quite a sight, with the backdrop of an industrial area and the working plantation in the foreground. I also stopped at Berkley Plantation, where Benjamin Harrison, a signer of the Declaration of Independence, lived and William Henry Harrison, his son and President, was born. William Henry Harrison was 69 when he was elected President. Some thought he was too old to be President. His inauguration was held on a cold spring day and to prove a point, he stood out in front of the crowd to give the longest inaugural speech ever without dressing for the 48-degree day with a cold wind. He died of pneumonia 31 days later. John Tyler became the first vice president to take over the top spot, so no one knew how this should be accomplished. John Tyler had no such doubts, being a Southern Democrat serving under a Whig President. He stood strong for states rights and American expansion. He made enemies and impeachment was even tried against him. His enemies knew him as His Accidency. He did get Texas annexed before he left office in 1845.

Sherwood Forest, John Tyler's home, is what I came to Charles City to see. The name came from the fact that John, with all his political enemies in Washington, felt like the outlaw Robin Hood. His home is 310 feet long to suit his second wife Julia's wish for a long ballroom to accommodate guests to dance the Virginia Reel.

John's first wife, Letitia, was sickly and died in the White House in 1842. In 1844, at 54, John married the 24-year-old Julia Gardiner. The couple loved animals, which the dog statues and pet cemetery attest to. John's horse, General, is buried here with the inscription, "General never made a wrong move; I wish I could say the same."

John Tyler, who was born in 1790, still has a grandson who lives in the house. Yes, his grandson. We could hear Harrison and his wife,

Painy, upstairs. Tim, our tour guide, even showed us their liquor bar. He said Harrison drank two glasses of white wine a day and the glasses keep getting bigger. There was also talk of ghosts messing with the lights and stairs. Harrison is 85. His father was 75 when he was born, and John Tyler was 63 when Harrison's father was born.

Tyler had picked out a burial site for himself on his property, but he seceded with the South and was a Congressman for the Confederate House of Representatives when he died in 1862, so he was buried in Richmond where his remains would be safe. The North did use his house for living quarters and even tried to burn it, but some loyal slaves saved it.

Later in the week, I visited President James and Dolley Madison's home in Orange, Virginia. Dolley was a widowed Quaker and James was a very studious, frail five-foot-six-inch guy with stomach problems and a voice so soft he was hard to hear. His mind was exceptional. I was in his upstairs study where he put together the foundations for our Constitution. Dolley loved red, which makes her a good person in my book, and she loved to entertain, which the pork bones from barbecues in the backyard attest to.

Friday night back in Fredericksburg, I didn't feel well. Sinus was kicking in, both head and stomach. Tea and Ibuprofen became my doctoring. Not knowing how the traffic would be on the 40-mile trip on I-95 up to Washington, I got going at 4:30 AM. I jumped on the Metro south of the city. It took 40 minutes to get to the Washington DC Rock-N-Roll Marathon race start area, time enough to think about what I've done and what I can expect on that Saturday. Back in February, I finished one of the hardest 50K Birkebeiners ever and in the top 1000. As part of the early Birchlegger Wave, we skied on a mostly ungroomed trail due to a 10 – 15 MPH wind blowing snowdrifts across our path. Fifteen days later I did the Lower Potomac Marathon in 4 hrs. and 39 min. Now six days after that, I'm trying another marathon with sinus firing and I forgot my sunglasses in the car. I better take it easy and not expect too much.

I arrived at the start area at about 6:30 AM. Time to get in the porta-potty line. Look one way and there is the U.S. Capitol, look the other way and you see the Washington Monument. It was a cloudy, cool day, probably in the lower 40s. The second time in the bathroom line, the lines were much longer, probably 50 or more people in each line.

When I got near the front, the woman ahead of me told the person in the next line to go ahead. I'm thinking, look at the people behind you before you are too generous.

There were about 30,000 runners and 500 to 1,000 of us were sent out in a corral at a time, every one to two minutes. I was in corral 18 so I didn't take off until almost 8 o'clock. I decided not to look at my watch, nor let other runners influence my pace. It was very crowded for the first half of the marathon so not letting other runners influence my pace would be difficult, especially when being competitive is engrained in me. After mile 13 the field really thinned out and the sun came out, which I didn't need. It seemed that every time we took another turn, we had another view of the capitol. There were a couple of fair sized hills toward the end. I decided I would save what was left in me and walk up two of them. With two miles to go, I decided to look at my watch and I had 29 minutes to break five hours. Soon I could see RFK Stadium and that meant the finish line wasn't far off. I finished in 4 hours and 57 minutes. I met my goals and now I have 49 states plus our nation's capital completed. It is time to go home. Out of those 30,000 runners who were part of this event, only 2,733 finished the marathon. I was the 2,141st finisher and 12 out of 26 in the 60-64 age group.

The Metro ride back to my car was kind of like a victory lap. I made it. Once I got to the airport, I couldn't pass up a burger and fries. Eating whatever looks good is a good feeling once in a while. I almost fell into the aisle while falling asleep on the flight home. The van driver taking me back to get my car had to make a stop at Mall of America. One of the six people who were picked up at the mall mentioned how tired he was. I thought to myself, you have no idea.

Mt. Vernon with George's sword
and Martha's wedding dress and
shoes in the insets

John Tyler's home where his Grandson Harrison and wife,
Painy, still live. Inset: The family pet cemetery where John's
horse, General, is buried.

Maui Marathon

Lahaina, Hawaii

September 19, 2014 Denise and I met our friends, Jim and Diana Heinz, at their home in Las Vegas before flying to Kahului, Hawaii. Jim and I were both doing the marathon. The flight took six and a half hours, the longest I care to ever be in a plane. As we left the mostly open-air airport in 90 degree Kahului to find our red rental Hyundai Santa Fe, we noticed chickens running all over the place. I later found out they got loose from a previous hurricane.

When we found our way out of the airport, we took the route of the marathon over to Lahaina to pick up our race packets. Denise decided against the Taco 5km because of the heat and humidity.

Now we had to find our condo in Wailuku, where we headed, with Jim and Diana's GPS locked in on the correct address. Seven miles from Wailuku, their machine told us we were nearing the condo location. Of course, a non-tech guy like me started arguing with the machine. Then I remembered that the condo was within walking distance of Ma'alaea Bay so I obeyed the machine and found the condo, but the office was closed. We started calling numbers to find out how to get in. The fourth number brought success. I pressed a code into a small vault to open it and inside was an envelope with our key and directions. I felt a little Magnum PI coming out.

Saturday we tried to adjust to the change of time and weather. The ocean was right out the front door, so we jumped right in. I even learned about the history of sugar cane at a local museum.

Sunday morning was an early start. We had to be at the Queen Ka'ahumanu Center in Kahului early for the 5 AM marathon start. It was already in the mid-seventies and humid.

The Japan Travel Bureau, the main sponsor, offered fruit kabobs and other fruit selections laid out for us. There was even a fire dancer putting on a show before the start. After the Japanese and US national anthems were played, we lined up and walked about three blocks to the start line. When we were ready to go, a sports car plowed right into the sea of runners. The driver was drunk and kind of rolled out of his car when the police arrested him. Everyone managed to get out of the way except one volunteer, who got a thirty-foot ride on the hood of the car with only minor injuries. The driver was hauled away and given a $1,200 fine.

The race finally was off on the predawn streets of Kahului. Once we got to the Kuihelani Hwy., the air seemed to move a little, with only sugar cane fields bordering the highway, but I could tell when the sun came up it was going to be a sauna. My glasses steamed up, so I went without them until the sun became an issue, and I drank something every mile. When the junction came with Hwy. 30, we were on our way to Lahaina and a long gradual downhill along Ma'alaea Bay. The sun was becoming a problem.

At the end of the long downhill grade was a hill section with a tunnel through the West Maui Mountains. This section was mostly shaded but I could feel the energy level going down fast as we got to the halfway point. It was flat and open now as we ran along the ocean. I got to mile fifteen and one of many aid stations. The volunteers were great. They gave me a chair to sit on for a minute and all the cold water, ice, and fruit I could eat. A teenager there wearing some kind of historical thong, said he was sweating in the shade and wondering how I could run.

At mile sixteen I was about three hours into the race and thinking survival. I figured the combination of running and walking would get me through the last ten miles in reasonable time for such an event. Some large trees hanging out over the road gave us some shade, but that didn't last. Then we headed off the highway through a residential district of Lahaina. It really got hot. We passed the sign for the Old Lahaina Luau where we were going in a couple of nights, but right now it was just a sign.

Finally the finish line came in sight. Denise asked the announcer to let the crowd know I was finishing my 50th state marathon. It took me 5 hours and 46 minutes, which would normally be slow, but the average finish time was 5 hours and 21 minutes so I was okay with that. I talked to one young lady runner over the last couple of miles and she said this was her slowest marathon but the one she was most proud of. I was the 486th to cross the finish line out of 748 finishers. Jim beat the eight-hour cut-off but he was hurting also.

After a couple of hours rest, Jim and Diana took Denise and me out to eat to celebrate completing the 50 states. Jim was close to completing the state marathons, also. He lacks three, two of which he plans on doing in October.

Before leaving Hawaii, we had to experience a little more of what Maui offers. On Monday we drove the very scenic Hana Highway, a winding road that increases in elevation and narrows to one lane quite often. The road is well traveled and speed can be an issue. Many times I found myself directing oncoming traffic from the driver's seat, especially where there was only one lane and someone had to give the right of way. It was much calmer when we arrived at Haleakala National Park and hiked the four-mile round trip to the four-hundred-foot Waimoku Falls through a bamboo forest.

Tuesday was Jim and my day to pick up our rented mountain bikes, drive to the top of Mt. Haleakala, and ride about twenty-five miles down the 10,023 ft. mountain. It was 58 degrees at the top with about a 20 MPH wind. The road was mostly switchbacks with several 15 MPH turns, one which we almost missed. I pedaled only twice all the way down. It must have been quite a sight, seeing a 74- year-old following a 62-year-old flying down the mountain on mountain bikes with full-face helmets.

Wednesday was snorkel day. Four crazy guys on the Mahana Naia catamaran took a bunch of us novice snorkelers out to Molokini Crater. The calm day allowed us to go around the back of the crater and watch marine life in the very clear waters, where you could see 120 feet underwater. Along with the coral reef and colorful fish, we saw a small shark. The crater still has an unexploded torpedo in it. The authorities don't want to explode it, in fear of sinking the crater. Later we went across the bay and watched the sea turtles, where they were most at home under the ocean. On the ride back to the dock, several dolphins escorted us in some fairly rough water. That evening it was time for the Old Lahaina Luau. Along with a great meal of Hawaiian dishes, including a traditionally roasted pig, Hawaiian history and culture was presented Hawaiian style in a great show. The Hawaiian culture appears to be very much alive, despite efforts of several countries to change it during colonial times.

The next day I tried surfing, a sport some people in our country at one time had tried to stop because the Hawaiians were having too much fun. A big Hawaiian named Al was our instructor. Three teenage girls and myself were the students. I held my own with the rest of the class and even made it all the way to shore. That was better than Mark Twain who tried it back in 1866 and almost drank the ocean, they say.

On Friday we flew home, after finishing the fifty states in style. The words of James Cook, the first European to lay eyes on Hawaii in 1778, seem fitting.

"Do just once what others say you can't do and you will never pay attention to their limitations again."

Outdoing Mark Twain at surfing

Halfway point of the Maui Marathon

One hot finish line

"If one has cut, split, hauled, and piled his own good oak, and let his mind work the while, he will remember much about where the heat comes from."

Aldo Leopold

This accomplishment is two years of wood, cut, split, and piled.

Lifestyle vs Training

As a teacher, running a race is something I can do where I can actually see the accomplishment. I start here and I end there. The medal at the end of a marathon becomes a little more visual reinforcement. With teaching, you try your best, but with so many variables, you're never sure how much is accomplished by your effort. Once I retired, running marathons still gives me a sense of accomplishment. Now that the fifty states are completed, it's time to set a new goal.

I hope to run a marathon in all thirteen provinces and territories of Canada. I have already run a marathon in Thunder Bay, Ontario and Winnipeg, Manitoba. I have eleven to go. I would like to run a marathon in Mexico so I will have run marathons in all North American countries. Finally, I'd like to run a marathon on the other continents, but I may leave Antarctica out. It is very expensive to get there and its lack of human history makes it unattractive to me. I already scheduled a marathon that includes part of the Great Wall of China.

To get ready for any event, I believe in making biking, running, and skiing a lifestyle rather than a training program. I do whichever of these sports the outdoors allows each day and I keep track of the total miles in each activity. Watching those miles pile up is a good motivator. Cutting, splitting, and piling firewood seems to be good upper bodywork. The effort pays off in lower fuel bills and I don't pay anyone for a training gym or equipment. I never run more than eleven-and-one-half miles at a time to get ready for a marathon. The marathon is long enough, without twenty-mile runs to prepare for it.

I like quoting people important to our history. I figure we have the greatest country in the world, so their words have meaning. Here is Thomas Jefferson: "Do you want to know who you are? Don't ask. Act! Action will delineate and define you."

So, I say set a goal and go for it. Completing the goal isn't the issue. Giving yourself purpose by going after the goal is.

Once again as my distant relative, Abraham Lincoln, rightly said: "It's not the years in your life that count. It's the life in your years."

Distant Relatives

50 States Completed

Marathon	Date	Time	Place
1) Grandma's Marathon	6/19/93	3hrs.29min	Duluth, MN
2) Taos Marathon	6/6/98	4hrs.13min.	Taos, NM
3) Paavo Nurmi Marathon	8/8/98	4hrs.13min.	Hurley, WI
4) Deseret Marathon	7/24/01	4hrs.21min	Salt Lake City, UT
5) Governor's Cup Marathon	5/31/02	4hrs.20min.	Helena, MT
6) Des Moines Marathon	10/6/02	4hrs.10min.	Des Moines, IA
7) Deadwood Marathon	6/8/03	4hrs.26min.	Deadwood, SD
8) Humpy's Marathon	8/17/03	3hrs.58min.	Anchorage, AK
9) Ozark Mountain Marathon	11/23/03	4 hrs 9 min	Branson, MO
10) Country Music. Marathon	4/24/04	4 hrs. 21 min.	Nashville, TN
11) Sunburst Marathon	6/5/04	4hrs.4min.	South Bend, IN
12) Mesa Falls Marathon	8/28/04	3hrs.59min.	Ashton, ID
13) Philadelphia Marathon	11/20/04	4hrs.11min.	Philadelphia, PA
14) Whiskey Row Marathon	4/30/05	4hrs.30min.	Prescott, AZ
15) Estes Park Marathon	6/19/05	4hrs.41min	Estes Park, CO
16) Run with Horses Marathon	8/27/05	4hrs.13min.	Green River, WY
17) Atlanta Marathon	11/24/05	4hrs.12min.	Atlanta, GA
18) Charlottesville Marathon	4/15/06	5hrs.9min.	Charlottesville, VA
19) Grandfather Mt. Marathon	7/8/06	4hrs.36min.	Boone, NC
20) Crater Lake Marathon	8/12/06	4hrs.43min.	Crater Lake N.P., OR
21) Gulf Coast Marathon	11/25/06	4hrs.54min.	Gulfport, MS
22) Eisenhower Marathon	4/7/07	4hrs.30min	Abilene, KS
23) Bayshore Marathon	5/2/07	5hrs.25min.	Traverse City MI
24) Route 66 Marathon	11/18/07	4hrs.27min.	Tulsa, OK
25) National Guard Marathon	5/3/08	4hrs.27min.	Lincoln, NE

26) Hatfield/McCoy Marathon	6/13/08	4hrs.32min.	Williamson, WV
27 Quad Cities Marathon	9/28/08	4hrs.49min	Moline, IL
28) Las Vegas Marathon	12/7/08	4hrs.22min	Las Vegas, NV
29) Glass City Marathon	4/25/09	5hrs.13min.	Toledo, OH
30) Discovery Marathon	6/7/09	4hrs.26min	Port Angeles, WA
31) Freedom Run Marathon	10/2/09	4hrs.42min.	Shepherdstown, WV
32) Space Coast Marathon	11/29/09	4hrs.25min.	Cocoa Village, FL
33) Fargo Marathon	5/22/10	4hrs.37min.	Fargo, ND
34) Lake Placid Marathon	6/13/10	4hrs.29min.	Lake Placid, NY
35) New Hampshire Marathon	10/2/10	4hrs.23min.	Bristol, NH
36) Mid South Marathon	11/6/10	4hrs.17min	Wynne, AR
37) King's Mt. Marathon	4/09/11	4hrs.25min.	Blacksburg, SC
38) Kentucky Derby Marathon	4/30/11	4hrs.42min.	Louisville, KY
39) Mt. Desert Island Marathon	10/16/11	4hrs.23min	Bar Harbor, ME
40) Rehoboth Beach Marathon	12/7/11	5hrs.53min.	RehobothBeach, DE
41) San Luis Obispo Marathon	4/22/12	4hrs.29min.	San L' Obispo, CA
42) Mad Marathon	7/8/12	4hrs.43min.	Waitsfield, VT
43) The Chosen Marathon	10/27/12	4hrs.6min.	New Braunfels, TX
44) Rocket City Marathon	12/8/12	5hrs.30min	Huntsville, AL
45) Ocean Drive Marathon	3/24/13	4hrs.27min.	Cape May, NJ
46) Cox Sports Marathon	5/12/13	4hrs.56min.	Providence, RI
47) ING Hartford Marathon	10/12/13	5hrs.5min.	Hartford, CT
48) Myles Standish Marathon	11/17/13	5hrs.21min.	Plymouth, MA
49) New Orleans Marathon	2/2/14	4hrs.53min.	New Orleans, LA
50) Maui Marathon	9/21/14	5hrs.46min.	Lahaina, HI
*) Washington DC Marathon	3/14/14	4hrs.57min	Nation's Capital
*) Lower Potomac Marathon	3/9/14	4hrs.39min.	Piney Pt., MD

Boston Marathon Qualifying Times 2015

Men's Age Group	Time
18-34	3hrs.5min.
35-39	3hrs.10min.
40-44	3hrs.15min.
45-49	3hrs.25min.
50-54	3hrs.30min.
55-59	3hrs.40min.
60-64	3hrs.55min.
65-69	4hrs.10min.
70-74	4hrs.25min.
75-79	4hrs.40min.
80+	4hrs.55min.

Women's Age Group	Time
18-34	3hrs.35min.
35-39	3hrs.40min.
40-44	3hrs.45min.
45-49	3hrs.55min.
50-54	4hrs.00min.
55-59	4hrs.10min.
60-64	4hrs.25min.
65-69	4hrs.40min.
70-74	4hrs.55min
75-79	5hrs.10min.
80+	5hrs.25min.

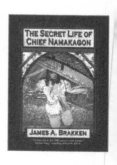

DARK - A CAMPFIRE COMPANION

56 very scary short stories & delightfully frightening poems. Spine-tingling tales of ghosts, dragons, ne'er-do-wells, and monsters—all waiting to raise goosebumps. Every story is morbidly illustrated by long-dead master artists of the macabre. Chilling, yet wonderful fireside reading. A "must-have" for every cabin bookshelf and home library. Ages 12 and up.

THE MOOSE & WILBUR P. DILBY
Plus 36 Fairly True Tales from Up North.

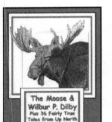

New! **Thirty-seven short stories straight from the heart & the heart of the north.** All fairly true, more or less. Some are sad, some shocking, most are hilarious. Small town tales of baseball, fishing, and hunting, tavern tales, jokesters, murderers, gangsters, and flimflam men. Lost treasure, lumberjacks, and legends of the north. Includes a 1-act play and several short stories based on the Chief Namakagon trilogy. Written for adults but fine for age 12. **Features *two* 1st place award-winning stories.**

SAVING OUR LAKES & STREAMS:
101 Practical Things You can do Today!

Whether lakes, ponds, rivers, or creeks, we love our waters. Cool, shimmering sheets reflecting sun, sky, and shore. Fish jumping, kids swimming, Man's best friend fetching. Our surface waters offer year-round pleasure to those who delight in their unique aesthetics. But, as we all know, our lakes and streams are at risk. Now, after more than two decades working with lake associations to protect and preserve our waters, James Brakken offers many of his articles and tips on practical ways we all can help save our lakes and streams. Brakken, a past-president of the WI Assn of Lakes and recipient of several conservation awards, shares his knowledge in an easy-going, non-confrontational, informative way.

Order the above books from
BADGER VALLEY PUBLISHING
Cable, Wisconsin 54821 715-798-3163
Free shipping from BadgerValley.com
Email TreasureofNamakagon@Gmail.com

Badger Valley can publish YOUR book, too!
Now accepting new book proposals!

To order additional copies of

DISCOVERING AMERICA ONE

MARTATHON AT A TIME

mail a check or money order payable to

Jim Anderson

42055 Cable Sunset Road

Cable, Wisconsin 54821

$15 cost per copy includes sales tax, handling, and shipping. All books ordered directly from the author will be inspected, signed, and promptly mailed.

Inquire about vendor discounts on drop-shipped bulk orders of 12 or more copies of any combination of Badger Valley books.

35613169R00100

Made in the USA
Middletown, DE
09 October 2016